SUCCESS HAS GEARS

Praise for Success Has Gears

"A book ALL present and future business executives should make required reading for ALL their department heads."

George A. Naddaff, Founder, Boston Market

"A thought-provoking guide to the dynamic process of leading in the modern workplace — even when you are simply leading yourself to higher levels of performance."

Greg Horn, Founder, CEO, General Nutrition Centers

"When you start a company, such as a software company, you need to shift gears from the day you come up with the idea until the day you sell the company, and the best employees are those that learn to shift gears with you. Collins and Israel have shifted down to make these concepts understandable, and shifted up to show us where they can lead.

Marty Schultz, Founder, CEO p2pLog; Co-Founder President and CTO, eSped and Omtool Ltd.

"Like most serial entrepreneurs, I've shifted gears more times than the lead driver in the Indianapolis 500. But it took *Success Has Gears* to create the map that shows business leaders not just why they need to shift gear but how and when to do it."

Seth Werner, President, Levitt Capital Corporation

"Three-Gear Leadership is the jet fuel that can propel an organization to the next level of sustainable growth."

Anita Brick, Director MBA Career Advancement University of Chicago Graduate School of Business

SUCCESS HAS GEARS

Using the Right Gear at the Right Time in Business and Life

**Susan Ford Collins
and
Richard Israel**

Book Two:
The Technology of Success Series

The Technology of Success
www.technologyofsuccess.com

Cover designs for The Technology of Success Book Series by Tim Kordik.

The Technology of Success
12040 NE 5th Avenue, Miami, FL 33161

Printed by CreateSpace

SECOND EDITION
ISBN-10: 0967191440
ISBN-13: 978-0-9671914-4-7

To the leaders of our next generation —
Cathy, Alan, Margaret, Steve, Lana, Susie and Ben.
We look forward to the ways you will enhance our world!

Susan Ford Collins and Richard Israel
2014

Contents

Foreword: The Workforce is Emerging—
But How About The Workplace?

Robert Morgan
President, Spherion Employment Solutions

Less than a generation ago, typical American workers put their fates in the hands of big organizations and essentially set their careers on autopilot. The employer did the rest. It told them when to come to work and when to go home, what to do and how to do it, when they would be promoted and when they would have to wait for advancement, how to dress and how to behave in the workplace. This was, for many employees, a predictable and relatively stress-free work life.

But a funny thing happened on the way to the 21st century, forever altering the lives and expectations of American workers.

For instance:

- Emergent workers feel more in control of their careers and want an employer that rewards them based on performance.

- Emergent workers define loyalty as how much of a contribution an employee makes.

- Emergent workers are more concerned with opportunities for mentoring and growth.

- Emergent workers want managers who are coaches and mentors who can help develop their careers.

- Emergent workers prefer a collaborative management style.

On the other hand:

- Traditional workers define loyalty as how long an employee stays with an organization.

- Traditional workers believe an employer is responsible for providing a clear career path and deserves an employee's long-term commitment.

- Traditional workers focus on job security and stability.

- Traditional workers prefer a more paternalistic management style.

This emergent mindset is becoming more and more prevalent in workplaces across the country. In fact, emergent workers now represent 31 percent of the workforce, up from 20 percent in 1997. And traditional employees make up only 21 percent of the American workforce, down from 34 percent in 1997.

Moreover, an increasingly plentiful segment of workers, nearly 50 percent, are classified as migrating from a traditional to an emergent mindset. If this trend continues unabated, which seems likely, Spherion expects that by 2007, 52 percent of the U.S. workforce will be emergent and only 8 percent traditional. Therefore, the new majority of employees will be emergent workers, while the traditional mindset will be all but extinct.

For employers that have moved toward an emergent style of management, this is good news. But for what appears to be the majority of employers, continued reluctance to "emerge" will make it increasingly difficult, if not impossible, to compete for talent. Difficulties will arise because of a growing mismatch between employees and employers, and that mismatch will be intensified by a growing labor shortage in coming years.

Who are these emergent workers? They don't wear signs. They're not located in one part of the country. They might not even respond to the term if they heard it applied to them. But their answers to questions posed by Spherion in 1997, 1999 and 2003 provide a clear and consistent portrait that sets them apart from their traditional counterparts.

These emergent workers wake up every day believing their destiny is in their own hands. They don't look to their employer to prescribe their development or manage their careers.

Emergent workers are not confined to any specific group. According to the study, they cross all boundaries including age, education, industry, size of company in which they work and level in the organization. These 21st century workers can be identified by new attitudes and expectations rather than by their demographic signature.

How Do We Deal With These Changes?

Authors Susan Ford Collins and Richard Israel look at the change we're confronting from another angle—an angle which not only spells out the challenge but also the solution. They show us that success and leadership have three essential gears. Like skillful drivers, we must be able to use all three gears at the right time, to not just reach the destinations other people have in mind for us, but also to reach the destinations we have in mind for ourselves.

Emergent workers are beginning to operate in the three success and leadership gears defined in this book. And the workplace they will want, and demand, will need to have leaders and structures that will meet their needs in these three gears. They will choose organizations in which their gears and their employers' will mesh...

- When they shift into 1st Gear to learn and relearn
- When they shift into 2nd Gear to produce and compete
- When they shift into 3rd Gear to create and innovate.

American workers are emerging quickly, but American companies are not. The majority of corporations, even new ones, are still operating in traditional ways. Here is the question: Will the workforce be able to find organizations where they can succeed, lead, and be led in all three gears? Will they be able to get the support and collaboration they will need to invent the next product or technology, the next method or system that will be needed and wanted in the workplace and world?

Those answers can be found here in this book. Written by two workplace experts, *Success Has Gears* shows corporations a way to meet the needs and expectations of the new American workforce. And it shows Americans how to prepare themselves to land satisfying, fulfilling jobs.

2013 Spherion Emerging Workforce Study

The most recent study found the following. Companies with well-developed brands/mission have a 70 percent rating for keeping current employees for the next 5 years, compared to just 34 percent for companies with no clear mission. Job satisfaction ratings are at 70 percent for those with solid brands, compared to just 23 percent for those without. 41 percent of employees working for a company without a clear mission are likely to seek employment elsewhere, compared to just 21 percent working for a company with a solid brand. Approximately one quarter of employees (23 percent) say their company does not have a clear corporate mission. Only 46 percent of respondents say their company is effective at communicating their corporate mission. And only 51 percent of workers say their company follows-through on their mission well. 41 percent of workers rate "a company whose online mission and values are followed-through upon" as important to their retention. 47 percent of workers agree that "when considering new employment, a company's online reputation will be equally important as the offer I am given.

Introduction: Success has Gears— and so does Leadership

A merica is in transition. In the pursuit of success and leadership, corporations, individuals and families across America are feeling tremendous pain—the pain of putting in longer hours, pushing harder than ever and still not being able to meet their needs. We are experiencing the loud, crunching sounds of old methods and structures collapsing around us, towns and their traditional industries shutting down, the mechanization of education and healthcare, ethics breaches, corporate scandals and greed. People planning to retire have been shell-shocked by losses in the stock market. Young families are caught in the dilemma of having to work so many hours that they have little time and energy left for raising their kids. Top producers are finding their hard work, instead of bringing riches, has resulted in poor health, divorce and fragmented, unhappy lives. Corporations driving for profits are cutting costs and people. More and more high-income jobs, and the spending power of Americans who used to do them, are being sent overseas. What is happening to us and why?

The Three Gears of Success

M ost people don't realize that success has three gear-like phases. **The 1st Gear of Success is starting or restarting.** You must shift into 1st Gear to learn new skills and information, to use new tools and technologies, to grasp the basics of new places, experiences and relationships. Whether it's your first time behind the wheel with your foot on the gas or sitting at a computer with your hand on a mouse, or you're starting over after a setback or failure or striking out in a new direction of your choice, in 1st Gear you feel like a kid again. Your emotions swing: excited/scared, safe/unsafe, trusting/distrusting, certain/uncertain, eager/about to quit. You know you don't know, and you need others to tell you specifically how, what and when. To succeed now, you must be willing and able to follow the beginner's rules and limits that your leaders believe will keep you safe as you learn.

The 1st Gear of Success was all too familiar to us as kids, but it's challenging for us as adults. How many of us stop to thoroughly read manuals or practice the basics of new skills before using them? But today we must be able to competently learn in 1st Gear to keep pace with the changes in information, tools and technologies that constantly bombard us. Once the limits of 1st Gear have been reached—once we are performing safely and effectively in this new area—it is time to gear up.

The 2nd Gear of Success is becoming efficient and competitive

Instead of sticking to beginner's rules, we begin taking shortcuts, dropping out steps and refining the methods we've been taught. The 2nd Gear of Success is about quantity, quality, winning, losing, budgets, charts, graphs, profit margins, raises, promotions, perks and bonuses. We work to produce more in less time at higher quality with fewer people. The mantra of 2nd Gear is more-better-faster-cheaper. But, as we continue to accelerate, increases in productivity slow down until we reach a point where no matter how long or hard we push, we can't produce any more, any better, any faster, any cheaper using the ideas, methods and systems we have in place.

The 3rd Gear of Success is creating and innovating

The shift to 3rd Gear comes when accumulated experiences and observations suddenly morph into invention and discovery, when an idea wakes us in the night or pops in mind as we're walking down a hall, taking a shower or driving. Interestingly enough, creative insights usually take place away from our desks. Aha! Wait! Stop! There's another way to produce this result—a different way, an easier way—and we're charged by our realization. This is the Shifting Point to 3rd Gear... if we can recognize and utilize it. But most people miss it. Why?

The shift from 1st Gear to 2nd Gear is usually decided for us by others—parents, teachers, employers and society. But the shift to 3rd Gear is one we must make ourselves. No one will be there to shift us, prompt us, or prod us. We must notice and respond, understanding the power of our idea and letting it guide us to implementation. These insights move our lives and our society ahead... when we are alert.

To operate in 3rd Gear, you will need to have the self-confidence to continue holding your dream despite day-to-day work pressures and the negativities of those around you who see this idea as impossible and proclaim so loudly. "No, that will never work." "What in the world are you thinking?" "You don't have the time, money, skill, experience, education, resources, or whatever, to do that." Their arguments will be convincing, sometimes more convincing than your dream at this stage in its development! If you fail to take action, your idea will fade from your mind... until you see on TV or online that someone turned "your idea" into a multi-million dollar product or system. That someone responded to an Aha! and invented Teflon, bar codes, Post-It Notes, ATMs, Amazon.com or eBay, until you realize you missed an opportunity to change your life and your world.

Leadership has three gear-like phases too

To succeed and lead, you must be able to recognize which gears those around you are in... moment by moment. Why is this Gear-Shifting Recognition essential? The leadership that individuals and teams require in each gear is different, quite different, as we will spell out for you in detail in this book. To improve your performance and the performance of your organization, you will need to understand which Leadership Gear is required and how to make the appropriate changes in your outlook and behaviors. To fail to do this causes short- and long-term pain, disruptions in our careers, our economy and our society. To fail to do this means failure.

Unfortunately, many of our leaders don't know which gear we should be in. Or which gear they should be in either. Today, too many leaders are overusing 2nd Gear, the more-better-faster-cheaper gear. Instead of shifting up and down as conditions require, they constantly race and rev in the name of productivity and profit. They train, promote, perk and bonus us to stay in 2nd Gear with them... at great cost.

We have other leaders who chronically overuse 1st Gear, drowning us in a sea of red tape, restrictive rules and regulations. In the name of control and loyalty, they fail to feed us the information we need. They limit our independence and prevent us from thinking for ourselves and our organizations. They demotivate us and retard the development of our careers.

We also have leaders who are so stuck in 3rd Gear that they can't gear down to communicate their ideas so we can move them into production. And they are unable to implement ideas we generate.

What happens when a society overuses the 2nd Gear of Success? When it rewards, promotes, perks, and bonuses 2nd Gear behaviors disproportionately? When most of its citizens spend the majority of their time operating in 2nd Gear? That is what we are seeing all around us. What are the unanticipated consequences? This overuse compromises skills, jobs, relationships, health, education, security and infrastructure. It pressures us to ignore the values and ethics of 1st Gear. It prevents us from asking, "What is the outcome we want?" and "How could we do this?" It squeezes out 3rd Gear innovation and discovery—the tinkering and puttering we need to keep our society alive, current, and economically viable. With so much 2nd Gear pressure, too few of us have time and energy left to honor our leadership roles at work, at home, and in our communities, to invest in the creative ideas and hunches we have and we need to develop.

Our definition of success is far too narrow today. We are unconsciously defining success as money, power and possessions. We've lost our balance as individuals and as a society. But success must be much more than that. To be meaningful, success must include health, security, education and satisfying jobs. Success must encompass rest, recreation and quality time with family and friends. Success must include time for creativity and dreams. To continue succeeding, each of us needs to re-define success to re-include all the vital aspects that make life fulfilling and worthwhile. To continue succeeding, we as leaders must learn to recognize the behavioral signals individuals and teams are sending and be willing and able to shift into the matching Leadership Gears.

When we drive a car, we have to use the right gear at the right time to move us ahead easily. When we don't, our car lurches and stalls. Most drivers rely on their car's "automatic transmission" to determine which gear they should use and for how long. Similarly, as we succeed and lead, we depend on our "societal transmission" to shift for us. We are taught early on to wait for our parents and teachers to tell us when we are effective enough or productive enough to gear up and when we need to gear down. As we move into our careers, we are taught to depend on our trainers and managers to shift for us, and our gear-shifting dependence is reinforced once again. But our "societal transmission" is not working properly. It was designed for a very different time and economy, and many of our familiar 1st and 2nd Gear jobs and institutions are lurching and stalling.

Relying on the 1st and 2nd Gears of Success and Leadership is not enough to meet the needs of our rapidly changing, global workplace. To continue succeeding, America and its people must transition from a One- or Two-Gear Society to a Three-Gear Society—a society that can use all three gears smoothly and seamlessly to meet current and future needs

We are feeling the symptoms of Gear-Shifting Errors all around us, and we need to learn how to recognize and correct these errors. Susan studied 1,333 middle school students and, surprisingly, almost half of them told her they didn't want to be successful! Why? Because based on how they saw their parents "succeeding"—always on the phone, constantly overloaded by emails, never able to satisfy their bosses, regularly disappointing spouses and families, never having time for friends and fun—these kids had decided they didn't want to be successful! And, as a result, they weren't fully engaging in school, or anything else. But it wasn't success they were avoiding. It was the overuse of 2nd Gear and the imbalance caused by underusing 1st and 3rd.

Today we must assume more responsibility for our lives than ever before. Like it or not, we are responsible for quickly identifying changes and potential opportunities, for devising new approaches and methods, for rapidly learning new skills and information, for creating and recreating our careers and taking care of our health. We must prepare ourselves to actively take on these responsibilities now... or be left behind. But are we?

The impact of the overuse of 2nd Gear is alarming if we look closely at our schools. As a nation, we are falling behind in education, a 1st Gear function in which we used to excel globally. "The percentage of Americans graduating with bachelor's degrees in science and engineering is less than half of the comparable percentage in China and Japan, and U.S. government investments are flagging in basic research in physics, chemistry and engineering," wrote New York Times columnist Thomas L. Friedman. "The rest of the world is catching up," said John E. Jankowski, a senior analyst at the National Science Foundation. "Science excellence is no longer the domain of just the U.S."

Are we so preoccupied with 2nd Gear Success and Leadership that we are failing to nourish those 1st and 3rd Gear essential elements — education and innovation — that made America great? We, Susan Ford Collins and Richard Israel, are concerned that we are failing as a nation, and the long-term impact will be painful unless we reverse this trend quickly and learn to succeed and lead in all three gears appropriately.

The Technology of Success: 10 Skills for Succeeding and Leading

As a young researcher at the National Institutes of Health, Susan had an idea that kept her awake at night. "What more could we learn if we studied Highly Successful People (HSPs) not just ill and dysfunctional ones? Are HSPs using skills the rest of us are missing, or misusing? If so, what are these skills and how can we teach them?" Susan proposed her idea at one of their prestigious weekly conferences but, instead of being excited, her colleagues all laughed. Undaunted, she silently vowed to make this research her life mission. And she has.

Susan spent the next 20 years shadowing HSPs... everyone from Buckminster Fuller to corporate heads, inventors, scientists, artists, educators, athletes, coaches and parents. She discovered they were using the same 10 skills consistently, the 10 skills she teaches in The Technology of Success. "Using all Three Success Gears" is the Second Success Skill. (For more on the other nine skills, read *The Joy of Success* and *Our Children Are Watching*.)

In 1983, Susan met Richard Israel who immediately recognized the importance of the skill set she had discovered. Ten years before, Richard launched The ABC of Selling which rapidly became a global operation and advanced the careers of hundreds of thousands of salespeople. Richard knew he was the perfect person to help Susan translate her skill set into a full-fledged training program. Together they began creating and testing formats and manuals and facilitated the first Technology of Success trainings for Coopers and Lybrand, IBM and Levitz Furniture.

Since 1985, Susan has been teaching *The Technology of Success* in major corporations, universities and organizations across the country. When all 10 Success Skills are used correctly, individual and team productivity, collaboration and creativity rises to the next level. And profitability rises with it. This powerful leadership and career advancement program has been used by corporations including American Express, Ryder System, Digital Equipment, Florida Power & Light and CNN.

"At CNN we have a steady stream of the world's best consultants coming through. Most produce excitement but after only a few months, things slip back to normal. But now, six months after Susan taught my staff her success skills, I am continuing to see improvement" wrote Lou Dobbs, President of CNNfn, Host of *Moneyline* and *Business Unusual*.

"I learned more in a matter of hours than from all the management, leadership and team-building trainings I've taken in 18 years. And it works in my personal life too" said Carl J. Flood, VP Worldwide Management, American Express.

The Technology of Success skill set is essential for start ups. It is equally vital when companies are vying in our competitive global marketplace, and when creativity and innovation are required to advance to the next level. These 10 Success Skills empower team members to move ahead together, instead of forcing one or more to leave and take their ideas and expertise, *and your ideas and expertise*, on to a competitor. Knowledge-base losses are far more expensive and time-consuming than providing 10 Success Skills training for your team.

Now that you have a basic understanding of the three Success Gears, let's look at how they are used... and misused... in real life situations.

"CEOs have called creativity the No. 1 leadership competency of the future."

The Creativity Crisis, Po Bronson and Ashley Merryman
Wall Street Journal Fri May 9, 2014 U.S. Edition

Part One

The 1st Gear of Success and its essential companion—

the 1st Gear of Leadership

A Year in the Life of a Top Sales Rep

I t was a peak moment. Bob McMillan had just returned from Pharmco's national sales convention where he was appointed to the President's Council and invited to speak on how to be a successful sales rep. Because of Bob's consistent high performance, he had won every mixer, toaster, bonus and trip, even one that landed Bob and his wife, via helicopter, on top of a volcano high above the clouds in Hawaii.

Bob and Ellen finally felt secure enough to start a family and had the long-awaited call from Ellen's doctor: She was pregnant. Elated, they took the steps they had been planning: They bought a much larger home and new a mini-van.

But a few weeks after the conference, Pharmco lost the contract with SMB, a major healthcare provider. The loss was over profit margins and had nothing to do with how well, exceptionally well, Bob had been servicing their account. But instead of backing the loss out of Bob's next year's numbers, knowing it would eliminate one quarter of his income, management tagged the usual 6% annual increase onto his sales quota and told him to make up the difference however and wherever he could.

Bob was staggered. Now just to make his numbers, he would have to produce a 31% increase! Six per cent was a stretch but 31% was outrageous — a goal he couldn't imagine reaching. He tried talking to his boss and director and proposed alternative approaches, but they accused him of having a bad attitude and reaffirmed their goal. Bad attitude! That really stung. Bob had always been seen as "positive and resilient." In fact, those were the words his bosses had included in past appraisals.

The next twelve months were tough. Bob had felt valued and heard when he was exceeding expectations. His manager's and director's doors were always open. But now he felt he would have to survive on his own. Bob sensed he was rapidly becoming upper management's personalized message that no matter who you are or how well you've done in the past, you have to increase your business 6% each year.

Each morning Bob pumped himself up and called on new accounts. He was bringing in business at a respectable rate, but the threat of not making 31% kept him up at night. A few months ago, Bob and Ellen were sure they could handle the expenses a baby would bring, but now, whenever they sat down to pay bills, they worried. A nervous Ellen asked, "What if your paycheck stops coming and all these expenses don't? Our mortgage and credit card companies won't care about the loss of your SMB account! The first and fifteenth will still roll around."

"How long can we last on my income and our savings?" she wondered. "What will happen if you lose your job and your health insurance?" They both knew that her company's health plan wouldn't provide adequate coverage for the baby. Their long-trusted assumptions of job security and 6% growth were feeling like empty promises.

Bob's relationship with his boss, Howard, continued to decline. Howard kept delaying his annual appraisal and when they finally did meet, instead of reaffirming his confidence in Bob and pointing out his progress, Howard was critical and clearly seemed worried. "You just aren't making enough calls. You aren't bringing in enough clients. What's your plan, Bob?" A few months later, his boss's feedback started to feel threatening. "Bob, unless you pick up the pace and get the job done, we'll be forced to find someone else who can."

A year passed and it was time for the convention again, but this year Bob didn't walk away with all of the prizes; in fact, he didn't take home any. His directors who had introduced him around last year seemed uncomfortable even talking to him. Did they know something he didn't? Was there a message they weren't telling him yet?

He couldn't wait for this convention to end! His mind kept making excruciating comparisons between this and previous years. And most devastating of all, this year's winner only exceeded his plan by 10%. On the way to the airport, he passed his director, Rick, in the hall. Rick didn't look up. Bob was in a daze all the way to the airport. When his flight was finally called, he gathered up his garment bag and lap-top and headed down the ramp to the plane.

What have you done for me lately?

Each Success Gear has a corresponding Leadership Gear... one that specifically meets the needs of individuals and teams operating in that gear... the 1st Gear of Success and the 1st Gear of Leadership, the 2nd Gear of Success and the 2nd Gear of Leadership, and the 3rd Gear of Success and the 3rd Gear of Leadership. Today most of us spend most of our time accelerating in 2nd, striving to climb up to the next title, position or salary level. And most of our managers are accelerating along in 2nd Gear with us. But what happens when circumstances force us to gear down to rethink and restart? Will our leaders notice our shift and be willing, and able, to gear down with us? Or will they press ahead in 2nd Gear... and miss the opportunity?

If our leaders fail to shift, the resulting Mis-Gear-Match can be expensive. It can not only retard the growth of our career and our enthusiasm but cost our company time and money... if we're let go or we choose to move to another company. Someone else will have to be interviewed, hired, trained, and sensitively led in 1st Gear again. Whether we are learning to use a new tool or technology, or we're gearing down because of an obstacle or setback, our leaders need to be able to recognize when we're in the 1st Gear of Success and adjust their expectations and behaviors to shift into the 1st Gear of Leadership along with us.

Until last year Bob was accelerating along in 2nd Gear, building his business and making money for Pharmco and his family. When they lost the SMB account, it hit Bob like an oncoming truck. Wham! He was in shock but his leaders acted as though nothing had happened. They didn't shift back into 1st Gear to offer him the advice, care, and support he needed. They didn't offer him the time, experience, and expertise that would have helped him. Instead, they continued racing and revving in 2nd, struggling to reach their goals and to satisfy their own bosses.

Like good drivers, they should have stopped to see if Bob needed help. They should have made time to support him in rapidly becoming productive and competitive again. And, if they had been truly interested in their company's success, they should have considered the enormous cost of having Bob take the knowledge and experience he'd gained at Pharmco into the open arms and minds of a competitor. But they didn't. And he did.

What would responsible leaders have done?

How would responsible leaders have behaved when they heard about the loss of the SMB account? As soon as they found out, they would have immediately asked Bob to meet with them. Let's imagine sitting in on the beginning of this meeting and listen to what is being said. "Bob, we've just learned that we've lost the SMB account due to pricing, and we know this is going to profoundly affect you and Ellen. That's why we've asked you to come in and think this through with us." "SMB? Whew, it sure will. What happened?" asked a stunned Bob. "We simply couldn't make the price point they insisted on. These things happen from time to time, but we don't want it to hurt you. We would like to help you lay out a new plan and rethink your goals for the upcoming year."

This kind of support would have been great, but it didn't happen. If they had immediately geared back with Bob, if they had looked at next year's goals with him and guided him to them, he would have felt that Pharmco's leaders were there for him, and he would have reached his goals and taken home some awards. And even if he hadn't, he would have felt good about his company and been a far more motivated and loyal employee in the future! But instead they lost Bob to a competitor who gave him the support he needed and made him number one in their company (with an inside track on all the moves Pharmco would probably make). Unfortunately, millions of valuable employees are being lost in just this way because companies fail to understand this crucial shift from the 2nd Gear of Success back into the 1st.

His managers should have asked Bob what he needed from them. They should have set interim goals so he could begin having successes again, successes they could acknowledge to lift his spirits. In situations like these, your company should be your support system. After all, you spend more of your waking hours at work than any place else!

Your company chose you from a group of competitive candidates. They trained you in the skills they felt you would need and supervised you as you learned how to implement them. They cheered and encouraged you during startup. But will they gear down to match your needs now?

If Bob's leaders had supported him in these unexpected circumstances, his wife would have felt better about Pharmco too. She would have had felt confident the situation would work out successfully and his leaders would be there for him in the future. Instead she told him how unfairly he was being treated and encouraged him to move on to another company — which he did.

Take a look at the Overview of the 1st Gear of Success, what we all feel and do whenever we need to start up or start over. Notice the words that signal when you, or someone you are leading, is operating in 1st Gear.

"While 72% of traditional workers feel that changing jobs could damage their long-term career advancement, Emergent Workers view job change as a positive step and the vast majority (95%) are eager to explore new opportunities. As one respondent put it, 'If my company is not willing to give me that room to grow, I'll find it somewhere else.'"

2003 Spherion Emerging Workforce Study

Overview: 1st Gear of Success—
Is this right? Are you sure?

You must shift into 1st Gear...

- whenever you learn new skills and information.
- whenever you learn how to use new tools and technologies.
- whenever you find yourself in new places, relationships or experiences.
- whenever life circumstances change drastically or unexpectedly.
- Whenever you are forced to or choose to start over

In 1st Gear, you feel like a kid again...

- dependent and needy.
- your emotions swing back and forth.
- safe/unsafe, excited/scared, trusting/distrusting, certain/uncertain, eager/about to quit.
- you know you don't know or you think you do know but you don't.
- you need others to tell you what, where, how and when.
- you must follow instructions and try new approaches.
- you must stick to Beginner's Rules and Limits in order to succeed.

1st Gear Word Signals: The following words let you know when you or someone else is operating in 1st Gear...

right, wrong, good, bad, should, shouldn't, can, can't, have to, must, always, never, possible, impossible, rules, limits, safe, unsafe, certain, uncertain, excited, dependent, anxious, eager, scared, trust, distrust, follow, question, try, fail, retry, values, standards, morality, integrity, rules, praise, supervision, correction, consistent, effective, competent, test, permit, allow, under control, needy, unsure, fear-driven, over control, rule-driven, bureaucratic, rigid, unbending, limited, resentful, angry, hostile, helpless, disinterested, withdrawn

These words give you a feel for what is most desirable—and most destructive—about the 1st Gear of Success, depending on how skillfully you use it.

When you're in 1st Gear, you need 1st Gear Leadership...

- someone beside you to answer urgent questions that constantly pop up. What should I do? Is this right? Are you sure? Oops, what went wrong? What should I do now?
- someone to give on-the-spot feedback: yes, no, smiles, frowns, thumbs up or down.
- someone to determine appropriate rewards and punishments.
- someone to make sure you and your self-confidence survive.
- a leader to deliver feedback positively. Ah, that was good. Yes, you did that right... or No, that didn't work. Here's what will work. Or, you did it right last time. Let's try again.
- a leader who believes you can succeed.
- a leader you have confidence in until you build confidence in yourself.
- a leader to take charge of your learning process and keep you safe and on track.
- a leader to feed you the skills and information you need step by step.
- someone who makes sure you experience a steady stream of successes.
- a leader who makes sure your corrections lead to successes.
- someone to test, grade, correct and recorrect you.
- a leader to determine when you are performing safely, correctly, consistently.
- someone to determine when you are ready for 2nd Gear independence.
- A leader who acknowledges that he or she is shifting you into 2nd Gear

1st Gear situations include...

- learning to drive or ride a bike.
- learning to use a computer or surf the Internet.
- learning to use new programs on your phone or computer.
- starting college or professional training.
- getting your license to drive, to sell insurance, stock or real estate.
- getting your license to practice law, medicine, acupuncture or anything else.
- learning to use your VCR or TiVo.
- learning to play golf, tennis, to lift weights.
- learning to use your car navigation system.
- corporate training programs.
- starting or restarting jobs or relationships.
- learning to read and interpret the fine print in contracts.
- responding to shocking changes... like right after 911.
- after death, injury, separation, divorce.
- after burn out, illness, or job loss.
- initiating new relationships.
- responding to joyous changes.
- getting married, having a baby.
- learning to cook and multi-task.
- learning to parent and still live your life.
- buying your first home and getting your first mortgage.
- learning to read the assembly instructions for new products.
- learning to do maintenance and repair around the house.
- learning the rules of a new company, condo association or community.
- learning to sell yourself and your ideas in your company.
- learning to negotiate increases, benefits, better working conditions.
- learning to use your "crap detector" to ferret out the truth.
- learning to recreate yourself when your job becomes redundant.
- learning to change your diet and lifestyle.
- developing an exercise program you can maintain.
- initiating a plan or dream.
- learning to get along with your boss and your work associates.
- learning what your customers want and how to serve them.
- learning to deal with the politics of your organization.
- getting a promotion and learning new skills and responsibilities.
- learning to retire and restart your life.

"Ultimately, business leaders will make our training programs the venture capital of the 21st century workforce.

Elaine Chao, Secretary of Labor

Andrew Was Evaluated on All the Wrong Things

Andrew had just walked out of his first semi-annual review since being hired. During the last fifty minutes, he had received the worst evaluation of his life. He was smarting with frustration and choking down anger.

Andrew had been outstanding throughout high school and college, and his first-choice company, ComTech, immediately hired him. Days later, ComTech sent his mom an enormous bouquet of flowers for Mother's Day and included a handwritten note on corporate stationery thanking her for doing a great job raising her son, and letting her know they were proud to have hired him. She was thrilled and so was Andrew. Saying his goodbyes to family and friends, he quickly packed up his life and moved three thousand miles.

The technical support training program in Phoenix had begun the day before. He was the last person to be chosen for this position and delays in paperwork held up his departure. On the second day of his customer service training, Andrew picked up his rental car, carried his bags to his third floor corporate apartment and then followed the directions to the training site. He felt behind already. What had he missed on day one? But his instructor assured him he would quickly catch up, and he did.

For the next eight weeks he studied day and night, foregoing his morning biking routine, getting behind in his favorite TV series, his dishes and his laundry. Instead, he crammed every detail he could on how their system and technology worked, how to locate information, how to track time and projects, and how and when he would be evaluated. Outside the classroom, Andrew met the people he would be working with and heard speeches by executives and directors. He was already feeling the heat of the competition he would face. The training was intense, demanding and all-consuming but, on the last day when the scores were posted, he was the top of his class.

The following morning, Andrew let out a sigh of relief as he headed for his newly assigned cubicle and got ready to begin taking actual customer calls. He tried to use everything he had learned in college and the training program, and when he noticed "holes" he did extra reading at night to fill them. His new job was overwhelming at first: quickly orienting to the caller's problem, collecting the necessary information and doing the appropriate research on all his new systems. For a newcomer, he was doing well and, according to his customers' surveys, they wholeheartedly agreed.

A week later, Andrew walked into his semi-annual evaluation expecting to be acknowledged for his outstanding start up. But instead, his boss told him in a harsh, angry tone that, as far as he was concerned, Andrew hadn't contributed anything to his team's productivity and he had given him the lowest possible score.

Andrew was stunned and tried to explain that he had been in training almost the whole time, that he had done everything they asked, that he had studied nights and weekends, that he had been the top of his class. But this only enraged his boss who dismissed him with a wave of the hand and rushed off to a meeting. "Andrew, I don't give a damn about what they taught you in that training class. You've been on my payroll for the last nine weeks and I barely see one week's production. In my organization you either produce results. Or you don't."

When Andrew recovered, he began asking around: What had other students in his training class received on their evaluations? What had their managers said in their feedback sessions? Their managers had evaluated them based on their performance in the training program. On how effectively they had completed assignments. On how well prepared they had been and how they had related to the people in the program. As new hires, they were not ready to be productive and competitive. But their managers knew that if their new employees performed well in 1st Gear, they soon would be producing and competing and contributing to their team's performance. They understood that, at this point, their new employees' task was to do a great job of 1st Gear... and not 2nd.

In fact, if Andrew had been evaluated by his classmates' managers, he would have earned the top evaluation that quarter. But he wasn't and he didn't, and that evaluation held Andrew back for three and a half years... until he asked his fourth manager for a raise and that manager stopped to see why Andrew who was consistently receiving high scores wasn't at a higher grade and earning more money. Until his fourth manager recognized the leadership error Andrew's first manager had made and caught him up in salary and grade. He kept Andrew from leaving ComTech, which saved them the cost of rehiring, retraining, and rebuilding an employee's knowledge base and experience.

What do you need from your leader in 1st Gear?

Andrew was at the wrong place at the wrong time because his manager was in the wrong gear at the wrong time. His manager wasn't wise enough to see what an asset Andrew would be to his team and his company and he cut him off at the ankles. Instead of evaluating Andrew on the one week he was on his team, his manager should have evaluated Andrew for the nine weeks he had spent in training and how well he had performed there. Andrew may have been on his payroll that quarter, but Andrew's job wasn't to produce anything at that point; it was to learn how to do his job correctly.

Andrew's nine-week training program was conducted off site so he never met his manager or knew his manager was until a week before his evaluation. Clearly there should have been communication going on between training and management regarding Andrew's progress and where he stacked up in his class. During our years in corporations, we've observed a phenomenon we call "The Silo Mentality." It occurs when departments operate in isolation and withhold information that is vital to other parts of their organization. For example, when Sales fails to inform Customer Service about an upcoming ad so their reps are caught off guard by an onslaught of customer calls about a product they don't know they're offering, much less how to support it. These miscommunications also occur between sales and production or, as in this case, between training and management.

Andrew was in a real jam and he didn't just sit there passively. He went to Personnel and explained his situation but, instead of recognizing the Gear-Shifting Error his manager had made, they told Andrew his manager was one of their top producers and there was nothing they could do. They clearly took his manager's side and they didn't go to his trainer either. When you're in 1st Gear and brand new at something, that's when you need the most protection and support, and Andrew's Personnel department didn't provide the support either. Andrew simply didn't receive the leadership he needed at this point in his career.

Andrew considered looking for another job or trying to transfer within ComTech, but his industry wasn't hiring. And he was unable to transfer within his company either because this initial evaluation made Andrew look undesirable. Fortunately, he did speak with some top people informally and, even though they didn't get involved at the time, they did keep an eye on Andrew... and his manager. That manager was fired several years later because of similar and even more inappropriate behaviors. But the negative impact his behavior had on Andrew's life and the lives of several other employees wasn't noticed. And wasn't corrected either.

As we succeed, we must be responsible for following instructions and for becoming efficient. But in 1st Gear our leaders are far more responsible than we are. They are responsible for teaching us the basics of our new job. And they must also remember: Our failure is their failure too, their failure as a 1st Gear leader.

"When the job market tightens, will your employees remain loyal?
Smart entrepreneurs are moving now
to keep their best workers happy."

Fortune Small Business

"Finding the right people, bringing them onboard, providing the proper
training and making sure they are assimilated and
developed are not tasks most companies are set up to handle."

2003 Spherion Emerging Workforce Study

Overview: 1st Gear of Leadership— Instruct, Correct, Praise, Be Responsible

As a leader, you must shift into the 1st Gear of Leadership...

When individuals are in 1st Gear, they expect their leader to...

- take responsibility for their safety and success.
- make time to develop a learning plan and lead them through it step by step.
- teach them the Beginner's Rules and Limits they need to use to perform safely and correctly in this new area.
- choose someone to replace you if you cannot fill this responsibility... a trainer, mentor, coach or teacher.
- make sure your stand-in shares your values and has the skills, experience and judgment required.
- stay in touch with her or him; give and receive updates and progress reports.
- make sure you know how your shared-student is progressing. Or if s/he is not.
- remember how you felt when you were learning something new or in a new situation.
- remember what you needed from your leader at that time.

As a 1st Gear Leader, you are responsible for...

- building and rebuilding their skill and self-confidence day by day.
- teaching them your values and mission up front.
- building their self-confidence so they don't become overly dependent on you, or find others to glob onto who may not provide accurate instruction or lead them astray.
- listening to their questions and confusions and providing additional information and details.
- supervising, giving feedback and acknowledging progress until they are performing the new skill safely, correctly, consistently.
- testing, graduating and... by all means...celebrating their successes with them.
- encouraging them to share new ideas and approaches with you.
- listening to their questions and confusions and providing additional information and details.
- providing the depth of understanding they need to succeed not just in 1st Gear but in 2nd and 3rd in the future.
- recognizing their fresh point of view may bring understandings and insights more experienced team members are too busy or too numb to notice... too worried about targets, deadlines, politics and appraisals to share with you.
- remembering when you're about to let an employee go, that the information and experience s/he already has, plus some additional training, may be more valuable than starting over with someone who looks good on paper or in a 30-minute interview but who needs more training too and may not get the job done any better in the end.

1st Gear Word Signals: The following words let you know when you or someone else is operating in 1st Gear...

right, wrong, good, bad, should, shouldn't, can, can't, have to, must, always, never, possible, impossible, rules, limits, safe, unsafe, certain, uncertain, excited, dependent, anxious, eager, scared, trust, distrust, follow, question, try, fail, retry, values, standards, morality, integrity, rules, praise, supervision, correction, consistent, effective, competent, test, permit, allow, under control, needy, unsure, fear-driven, over control, rule-driven, bureaucratic, rigid, unbending, limited, resentful, angry, hostile, helpless, disinterested, withdrawn

These words give you a feel for what is most desirable—and most destructive—about the 1st Gear of Success, depending on how skillfully you use it.

If progress is slow, find out...

- if s/he is in too many 1st Gear situations at once... a new position, a new company, a new city, a new marriage, a new home, a new child.
- if this person, or someone close, is coping with illness or pain, death or serious loss.
- if this person is eating, resting and exercising in a healthy way.
- if this person has a solid physical, emotional and educational foundation in place.

Someone is unable to succeed in 1st Gear...

- when s/he can't or won't imagine succeeding in this area.
- when s/he consistently fails to follow directions.
- when s/he refuses to listen and follow through.
- when s/he lacks the skills, knowledge and aptitude to do this task or job.
- when s/he has always been told what to do.
- when s/he was taught to nod and agree but not allowed to participate.
- when s/he was not allowed to ask questions or make mistakes without punishment.
- when s/he is expecting you to lead that way too or feels you are even if you aren't.
- when s/he has such low self-esteem that, without major intervention, s/he simply cannot safely move ahead in this direction.
- when you must choose a new person to perform this task, responsibility or job.

"The illiterate of the 21st century will not be those who cannot read and write, but those who cannot learn, unlearn, and relearn."

Alvin Toffler, futurist and author
Future Shock

Mighty Mike: Hungry to Make Money

A t 56, Phil Johnson was frustrated and worried, frustrated that with a Masters Degree from a top university and 30 years experience in PR, he found himself unwanted, and worried that last year he sent out 150 resumes which resulted in five interviews but no job. His funds were running out. If it wasn't for his wife Audrey's position as a loan officer, they would have burned through their savings months ago.

"What can I do to make a living?" Day and night that question plagued Phil. And the feedback he heard from interviewers didn't help either. They kept telling him that he was too old for a full time corporate job. But, with seven years to go until Social Security and Medicare kicked in, he had to find something... and hopefully something with benefits.

Several months ago he joined a career change support group, but it was his wife, Audrey, who came up with the idea that worked. She reminded Phil that he loved to work on cars. He had more skill than their mechanic and, if he followed his passion, he could find a job in that industry. "What would I do with cars?" he charged back. "Sell 'em," Audrey concluded. "In good times or bad, people need to buy cars."

The thought of being "a car salesman" was his biggest barrier up front. He and Audrey discussed his feelings at length. "What would my family say if they knew I was selling cars? My poor mother would die... or cry." "Cry about what?" Audrey fired back. "Cry because you're out making a living? Put your ego aside and go find a job. We both know you can do it and God knows we need the money."

It took less than twenty minutes for Phil to skim the classified section of their local paper and circle six ads that all said the same thing: "Experienced Car Salesman Wanted. Write your own check. Work your own hours. Commission only." For a few minutes Audrey and Phil sat in the warm glow of believing they had found an answer and money would soon be coming in again.

Phil's background in PR provided the keywords he planned to use in the interview. When his interviewer asked him, "Why do you want to sell cars?" he would reply honestly, "Because I'm hungry to make money." Walking onto a neighborhood car lot, he quickly spotted a sign that said, "We sell NEW reconditioned cars" and his "hungry to make money" pitch hit its mark. The sales manager Mighty Mike's eyes sparked and he immediately shouted, "You're hired."

Mighty Mike was true to his name, all 280 pounds of him. His huge frame shook as he wise-cracked "Give me five," and his salesmen all slapped their hands against his extended giant paw. At their Monday morning motivational session, all seven salesmen sat around with drooped shoulders and freshly ironed shirts, sipping sweetened black coffee from chipped enameled mugs. "New day, new man," Mighty Mike said pulling Phil to his feet. "Give him five," he roared and they went through the motions. Mighty Mike told Phil they worked on the "up system" which meant you had to wait your turn to approach a customer. "What do we think when a customer tells you 'just looking?'" And they all answered in unison, "They're going to buy, buy, buy. "Give me five," shouted Mighty Mike jumping to his feet. Walking out of the sales office with one hand on Phil's shoulder and the other stroking his glossy silk tie, Mighty Mike chanted, "You're going to do just great here, yes sir, just great." As they ended their conversation with the obligatory high five, Phil was concerned this might be all the training Mighty Mike planned to provide. And he was right. Mighty Mike was a hell of a salesman but he didn't know the first thing about leadership.

Phil's first day at work consisted of hanging around, shooting the breeze, and waiting for his turn with a customer. Traffic was slow on Mondays and after ten hours, Phil headed home without so much as a nibble. But he wasn't discouraged. It had been new and exciting and his associates had told him amazing stories of untold riches that had been made on this very car lot. By the end of his first week, Phil had put in 60 hours. He had seen four customers… three just walked off and he'd TO'd (turned over) the fourth to Steve, their "number one closer," who couldn't close that one.

Late Saturday night Mighty Mike called Phil into his office. "Philly", a term of endearment Mighty Mike had made up for him, "Philly, in this business you have to sell, sell, sell and you haven't sold, sold, sold. But you're brand new and I'm going to give you another chance. Go home tonight and thumb through your address book, call your friends and family who have money, and get them to come in and buy a car from you." His frame shook as he chuckled at his own advice. "Philly, give me five." Phil hung on for another week with no sales and no paycheck. Then Mighty Mike let him go declaring, "Philly, you're burning the customer base." And, according to Steve, that meant he wasn't closing the walk-ins and so he was taking opportunities away from the real closers like him.

The following week Phil applied to a foreign dealership across the street. This time things went far better. International Motors had a three-day training program for new hires. Their program spelled out the rules and regulations of the dealership—how the various departments worked from service to finance. And, most important of all, it included two full days on the basics of selling cars. His new sales manager, Harry Upton, answered his questions and made him feel at home.

Next Phil was told to shadow (that is, follow around) Sam Spiegel, a high-integrity salesman with 20 years experience. Sam was great. He explained the ins and outs of the dealership and how to effectively sell their specific brand. He provided constant supervision and walked Phil through the paperwork until he was sure of it. With Sam's help, Phil put together the pieces of his new job like a giant jigsaw puzzle. His confidence was growing. He felt good about the dealership and the quality of the cars and service his customers would be receiving. And by the end of the second week, Phil had sold two cars. It was a start in the right direction and Audrey was delighted.

Who failed: Phil or Mighty Mike?

What a difference a leader makes! Mighty Mike expected Phil to "sell, sell, sell" but he didn't realize that he had to gear down to teach, teach, teach.

The quality of leadership is most important in 1st Gear when we're starting. Remember what happened when Phil left the first dealership and headed across the street. Harry started Phil off slowly, teaching him the ins and outs of his company and its divisions as well as the basics of selling their cars.

Phil's wife played a powerful leadership role in the development of his new career. It was masterful how Audrey shifted gears with Phil. She geared down to face the problem head on: They needed income and he needed a job. Then she geared up to devise a creative solution: Do something you love. And she recognized that the solution was selling cars. Next she overcame Phil's objections when his ego got in the way… me, a car salesman! Step by step, day by day, she guided her husband from feeling stuck and confused to sustained goal-directed action and income, even though it was uncomfortable for him and for her.

Then his mentor Sam Spiegel stepped in to provide the additional knowledge and self-confidence Phil needed. Their gears matched perfectly — the 1st Gear of Success and the 1st Gear of Leadership. Phil was well-prepared to produce in 2nd Gear, and he did. This is the kind of leadership that will be needed by millions of Americans who will be starting or restarting their lives and careers in the years ahead.

As adults, we sometimes forget how important it is to have a skillful leader beside us when we're brand new at something. Like when you had your learner's permit and your dad, mom or driver's ed instructor sat in the passenger seat next to you answering your thousands of life-saving and car-saving questions: Will this car fit between those cars up ahead? Can I parallel park in that space? When should I start braking? Asking these questions sounds silly to us now because as experienced drivers, these judgments are programmed in our brains. But when we were learning, they weren't there and we needed someone more experienced to fill in our holes in knowledge, experience and self-confidence. And to take responsibility for our safety and wellbeing until we are able to.

When we are leading in 1st Gear, it's important to shift into our own "starting something new" mindset—the mindset we were in when we first learned how to use a computer, surf the Internet, scuba dive or sky dive. If we fail to make this mindset shift as leaders, then we mistakenly assume that these tasks are as easy for them as they are for us. We underestimate difficulty and timeframes. Or we assume that others have the experience and decision-making abilities we have. We catch ourselves thinking, "Come on, that's easy" or "What's wrong? Are you stupid"? No, they're not stupid. They're simply new and inexperienced. They're simply in 1st Gear.

When we're learning and relearning, we need our leaders to believe in us. If they can't imagine us succeeding at this job, task or skill, it will be impossible for us to put our confidence in them until we can build self-confidence. In 1st Gear we need to know that our leaders have the time, skill, ability and willingness to get us from not knowing to knowing, from failing to succeeding, and ultimately to leading others to success too.

"The task of the leader is to get his people from where they are to where they have not been."

Henry Kissinger

Marvin on Monday Mornings

The chairs squeaked as the staff in the state office of Jobs and Benefits sat waiting uncomfortably for the meeting to begin. Four seats were empty when their office manager Marvin started, "OK, the first item on our agenda is lateness. Please note, this meeting was scheduled for 9:00 and people are still missing at 9:15. This is wrong, people. This is wrong." Their faces never moved. They were sick and tired of hearing the same ole, same ole, and they knew none of them would be there except for the paycheck.

Running Jobs and Benefits should have been simple. There was a clear set of rules and regulations to follow so that everything would run smoothly. But something deeply-rooted in the staff's psyche that could be summed up in one word... resentment... was blocking it. They resented that they were earning $1250 a month while their peers in the private sector were earning two or three times more. They were tired of driving old cars, wearing old clothes and counting every penny. They were sick of threats from "the powers that be in the state capital" to cut their budgets once again. They hated the endless rules and procedures that governed their every move.

"We must start and end on time. Coming late and leaving early is grounds for dismissal." They all knew Marvin was powerless to enforce what he was saying so his words fell on deaf ears. "People, clean up after yourselves when you use the kitchen. Also, someone has been eating Margo's lunch. No, this isn't funny. Margo left her sandwiches in the refrigerator twice last week and somebody ate them." Chuckles could be heard in the room followed by this suggestion, "Margo, next time, how about putting some poison in your sandwich so you can catch that rat." And Marvin continued, "If you are using your car for official business we must have accurate paperwork in order to reimburse you." "What do you mean if we are using our cars? Are you suggesting state-owned vehicles are available to us?" Chuck blurted out, and more laughter ensued.

The same complaints were heard week after week and never a mention of doing a good job. Just stick to the rules, do your work and keep your nose clean. "Please people, park your cars in the back and leave the front spaces for clients. And once again, I shouldn't have to tell you there's no, NO smoking in the offices. If you have to smoke, go out back and only one cigarette please. Last week I found people outside who don't even smoke. If you're a smoker, sign up on the Smoking List so I know who you are," Marvin added to more snickers.

"Now, here's an urgent matter. People, I have the numbers from the capital for last month's performance, and they're not good. Placements were down and the number of visits to prospective employees was down too," Marvin charged. "What's going on people, what's going on with you?"

"But, Marvin, how can we compete with recruiters in the private sector? They're impeccably dressed with company cars, leather briefcases and laptops, and we look like a bunch of hobos nobody takes seriously," Dan, the most outspoken member of the team, blurted out. "If they paid us a decent salary we could dress sharper and feel better about ourselves. But instead, we're the working poor." "Dan, you know the rule. We do not discuss salaries at these meetings," warned Marvin. "As a state agency, we don't charge employers for finding jobs. Providing this free service should be our incentive." There was a stony silence in the room. No one bothered to answer. What's the use, they concluded. "Please people, we must improve our performance," Marvin whined.

The meeting ended. Some associates wandered back to their desks while others headed to the kitchen to refill their oversized coffee cups. Doris, who'd been with the department for 15 years, went to speak with Mark in his cubicle. "Have you read this article in *The Daily News*?" she asked and she laid the paper on his desk. "Nope," replied Dan. "Then you definitely should. It's from an insider who says the state is planning to close our division next year," explained Doris. "Oh really, and where will the unemployed masses go for help?" he volleyed back. "The article says Lockheed Martin does what we do in other states and they're having talks at the capital," Doris replied. Dan scanned the article quickly. "This is scary," he concluded, "Very scary. Well, you know the story. We need updated computers, faster internet connections, more phone lines and furniture. But there's no budget for upgrades and so we keep slipping farther and farther behind the times," Doris asserted.

"Dan, why don't we start a recruiting business of our own? Between us we have the knowledge and experience we need and we know all the local employers." Dan thought for a moment and responded wistfully, "You're right, Doris, you know. But it takes capital in a capitalistic system and we don't have any."

"Perhaps we should be pushing harder for change," Doris mused and Dan cut in, "If we had decent leadership that might make a difference. But enough already. You and I could spend the rest of our lives debating this issue. I've got calls to make," Dan said ending the conversation.

Days, weeks, and months dragged by with nothing much to report. Oh yes, there was increased absenteeism. People showed up with fake doctors' certificates. Someone stole the equipment from the training room but a police investigation led nowhere. And at the end of the year Marvin ruled no alcohol would be allowed at the holiday party because things had gotten unruly last year. And somebody told him to go screw himself.

Soon after New Years, an article appeared in *The Daily Times* announcing that a private company had won the bid to take over Jobs and

Benefits as of March 1st. And months later, it was over... no more department, no more Marvin and no more squeaky chairs on Monday mornings.

Train him or replace him. He's stuck in 1st Gear

Here's a leader who is clearly stuck in 1st Gear. And who is trying to keep his staff stuck there with him. He's bureaucratic and unbending. He wastes his time and that of his staff members' on his constant attempts at control without providing the 2nd Gear and 3rd Gear Leadership that would empower them and him. And we know just how his team feels. We've seen corporate bosses and teachers behave the same way. And even say the same things. That's why you probably laughed as you read this story. Because it's true.

What can you do when you find yourself in a situation like this? All too frequently the only solution is to build your self-confidence in other areas of your life, look for something that suits you better and move on. Over time the marketplace will eliminate organizations that are stuck in 1st Gear. Take the post office, for example. Little by little their customer base has been nibbled away by FedEx, UPS, Postal Plus and email. But now they're gearing up and implementing creative changes.

How many departments across the country are caught in this gear-shifting dilemma? Some leaders and organizations don't allow their employees to shift into 2nd Gear productivity or 3rd Gear creativity. Instead they starve their confidence and enthusiasm with a steady diet of restrictive rules and regulations, backward systems and inadequate pay.

Sad to say, early on those employees shifted themselves into 2nd Gear hoping to get additional rewards for their productivity. And, yes, they shifted themselves into 3rd Gear to devise creative solutions. But when their attempts were not rewarded, when they were laughed at and even punished, they moved on to more rewarding and fulfilling positions. Or they gave up and stayed for the paycheck. They comply and do the minimum, poking fun at their bosses and "the system" to stay sane and functional. But we regularly see stories on TV about usually-quiet, hardworking, rule-following people who can't take the limits of 1st Gear anymore and go ballistic, turning their anger against co-workers and themselves.

Dan said that leaders above Marvin knew he was the problem and didn't do anything about it. That's how it usually is. What could they have done to turn this organization around? If we want individuals to operate in 2nd and 3rd, then we have to make sure they have leaders who reward them not just for following and sticking to rules but for 2nd and 3rd Gear behaviors as well, for being productive and competitive and being creative and innovative. Marvin needs to be retrained and reevaluated on his ability to succeed and lead in all three gears. And, if he cannot, or will not, his managers need to let him go and find someone who can and who will. *Organizations — government, corporate or community — cannot afford to lose their viability because a leader is stuck in one gear, whether that gear is 1st, 2nd or 3rd.*

M. A. Rosanoff: "Mr. Edison, please tell me what laboratory rules you want me to observe."

Thomas Edison: "There ain't no rules around here. We're trying to accomplish somep'n!"

Just the Girl Next Door

Julie White was just like the girl next door, the one you grew up with, went to school and fell in love with. To look at Julie, you would never have guessed that she was unsure of herself, but she was. Julie's father walked out suddenly when she was eight and was never heard from again. Her mother never recovered from this devastating loss, Depressed and withdrawn, she was unable to support her daughter as she was growing up.

Before he disappeared, Julie was daddy's little girl. He constantly told her how beautiful and smart she was. He told her what to do and she always did it perfectly. Without her dad and mom available, Julie was unable to find the validation and structure she needed. When people praised what Julie did, she was happy and all smiles. But when they didn't, she was unsure and depressed. Julie's childhood needs in 1st Gear were not met and she continued to search for someone to validate and love her. Her childhood lack of leadership set her up for adult disaster.

At 19, Julie landed her dream job as a stewardess for one of America's major airlines. At first it was exciting and new – the cities, the places, the adventures. Her supervisor, Jean Berwick, was filling the leadership void in her life, supervising Julie closely and providing constant support and feedback.

Six months later, Julie was flying and Jean was preoccupied with downsizing and union issues and couldn't keep up with the emails Julie kept sending. There was nothing urgent in them; just a constant need to touch base. The other stewardesses Julie trained with were thriving, but, for Julie, the thrill of new cities and exotic adventures soon lost its luster. She discovered she preferred sameness – the same home, the same food, the same daily routine. Without it, Julie was struggling to eat balanced meals and exercise regularly to keep up her spirits. Julie wasn't making a lot of money either. After deductions, her take home pay barely covered her bills with nothing leftover for emergencies and dreams.

To make matters worse, Julie saw a story in the newspaper saying that the president of the airline had set aside $27 million for his top executives' pension funds. He told the paper he'd been forced to do this to keep his key people. The employees were outraged. How could their president skim $27 million off the top when the airline was struggling to survive and management was constantly pressing the union for concessions? The big guys were being taken care of, but what about the little guys – the ones who were working and struggling? Employee faith in their president quickly vanished, and it was every man for himself… or herself.

Julie was flying the Miami-Bogotá run. Twice a week she laid over at La Plaza Hotel in Columbia. After checking in Monday and Friday evenings the crew met at the coffee bar before heading out for dinner and a nearby club to enjoy some local music. The town came alive at night and U.S. dollars went a long way.

One evening at the coffee bar, Julie met Ricardo. He was a good looking local artist who also played guitar. Their relationship was innocent enough at first. Ricardo always greeted Julie with a warm smile and a small gift. They had coffee, cake and an occasional walk. Weeks later, they started eating dinner together regularly. After three months they became lovers. Then it wasn't long before Julie was head-over-heels in love.

Meanwhile in downtown Bogotá, the traffic was so deafening that Raphael Mendoza had to walk over to close the window in his law office before continuing to speak. "I had a visit from upstairs," he told Marco who was sitting across from him, blowing thick blue smoke rings from a hand-rolled Cuban cigar. "What do they want this time?" Marco growled back.

"The U.S. is putting pressure on the Big One again. Some Washington congressman wants to know why we can't stop the drug trafficking, given all the money they keep pumping in. We need to sacrifice a mule." responded Raphael.

"How much and where?" Marco asked, inhaling deeply. "Say 20 pounds, through New York or Miami," Raphael mumbled. "I'll let you know," replied Marco. "Good. That'll will keep 'em off our backs for another six months," sighed Raphael as he turned to leave.

Julie's relationship with Ricardo continued to deepen. He was the father figure Julie had been longing for. He listened to her, advised her and provided understanding and praise. Soon he started talking about marriage and her head began to spin. "But we'll need money to get married," he reminded her. He was broke and she had only managed to save $2000. "Well, my friend Marco has connections," Ricardo added. "He can arrange for you to take something into the U.S. and make $30,000 in one day." "You mean smuggling?" she gasped in horror. "No, I mean making money for our life together. You work for the airline so it'll be a breeze."

Julie thought about it all night. "Ricardo was right. No crew members had been stopped by customs during the time she'd been flying there and the customs officers all liked her. Those greedy executives took care of themselves. Why shouldn't I do this, just this one time, so Ricardo and I can have a good start?" She told Ricardo to contact his friend Marco. Later Marco called Raphael who was brief and to the point. "The mule is running, Tuesday, 413 to Miami, White."

Two days later, Sam Michaels was reading *The Miami Herald* at the breakfast table while his wife Rose was cooking eggs sunny side up for him. "They caught another one," he read out loud with a sigh, "A 24-year-old airline stewardess was arrested Tuesday at Miami International with 20 pounds of cocaine in her flight bag." "What a shame," said Rose. "She's such a young girl." "Well, my kind-hearted lady, I'll try to find out what I can for you," Sam promised as he kissed Rose goodbye and headed for his office.

At the Rotary lunch three weeks later, Sam sat next to Dave Williamson, the Union attorney who had represented Julie in court. "There wasn't much we could do for her," said Dave. "She was caught red-handed. Yes, of course she was set up but try telling that to the judge and jury. Even though it was her first offense and she had excellent character witnesses, she still got eight years," Dave said disheartened.

"Why does our government let criminals, like these, prey on naive individuals? Julie goes to jail, and they keep drug trafficking and collecting money from our government to boot," Sam grumbled. Dave replied sadly, "It seems we have more greed than ethics these days. Unfortunately a girl like Julie is an easy target. When are we going to start looking at the real source of these problems?

What her leaders missed

Let's think about what Julie and her leaders might have done differently. Her supervisor, Jean, may have overlooked some important cues. She probably realized that Julie was more dependent than other employees she had trained, that she needed significantly more time, feedback and direction. Jean had probably heard Julie's story about "her dad's disappearing and her mom never recovering" more than a few times. Perhaps Jean had had concerns about how well Julie would do traveling in and out of foreign countries too.

Work pressures may have been Jean's reason for not taking action, but when she realized Julie wasn't confidently up and running in 2nd, she needed to gear Julie back down into 1st again. To stop and reevaluate her progress and her responsibilities. Perhaps she might have encouraged Julie to accept a position closer to home or in a place where she had a solid support system. Jean had probably heard about Julie's Colombian boyfriend, but she didn't make time to find out more, or feel it was her responsibility to do so. And technically it wasn't. But morally it might have been.

This is an extreme case, but it makes an essential point. Leadership is like a relay. The errors of one leader are passed on to the next: The errors of parents are passed on to teachers. If teachers fail to correct them, they are pushed ahead to employers. If employers don't handle them, they are conveyor-belted along to welfare, unemployment, law enforcement and correctional facilities around the country, and around the world. The effects of 1st Gear holes become more and more damaging and more and more expensive as time goes by. And they are frequently passed on the next generation as they were in Julie's case.

We have been focusing on her supervisor, but how about Julie's teachers? What did they notice and fail to correct? Did they recognize that Julie's self-confidence was low and she was more needy and dependent than other students? Were they aware of what was happening at home with her father and mother? I suspect they were.

Not all adults are grown up inside. When they are not, they need leaders who will create plans to address their needs so they can gear up to productivity, or, gear down to change their responsibilities so they are safe and they can contribute in their own way. Perhaps Julie would have been happier and safer checking people onto flights at her local airport. Whether she realized it or not, Jean was responsible for Julie, and so were her teachers and parents. And so is our society.

The cost of neglected 1st Gear needs is increasing the cost of healthcare, decreasing the ability of schools to prepare students for life, forcing business and government to handle needs that parents, schools and training departments don't have time, money and skills to provide. The costs of neglecting 1st Gear needs are passed on to each and every one of us.

Now Julie's lack of 1st Gear readiness will impact the whole airline. Captains will regularly remind crews that their airplane could be impounded and the company charged millions of dollars if any of them are caught bringing illegal drugs on board. Customs inspectors will look at every airline employee with suspicion.

Remember: Health and safety come first in 1st Gear

Simply giving people 2nd Gear independence doesn't mean they can handle it. As leaders, like it or not, busy or not, we must watch and ask,: are they taking responsibility for themselves and confidently producing in 2nd Gear? Or are their repeated requests for assistance and attention a cry for help—a cry for 1st Gear Leadership? Or a different job?

"As children grow, the baton of their leadership is passed from one leader to another. Teachers expect parents to have taught basic life skills, confidence and discipline. Businesses expect teachers to have developed academic, team and communication skills. Governments expect parents, teachers and businesses to produce individuals who can be healthy, responsible, successful citizens. But what happens when the baton of leadership is dropped along the way? When children who need skillful leadership fail to get it? How will they pass on what they were never taught? We can no longer afford to allow success and leadership to develop accidentally."

Susan Ford Collins
Our Children Are Watching:
10 Skills for Leading the Next Generation to Success

The Barron Family in Need of a Leader

Sunday dinner is supposed to be a family affair announced Bud as he grabbed a cold beer from the refrigerator and sat down to enjoy a hot meal from Boston Chicken with his wife Donna. "So where are the kids?" he asked. "Babs slept over at a friend's house and Chuck is at work," she responded. "Working on Sunday!" Bud shouted immediately. "Well, you told him that if he wanted his own car he would have to pay for half of it," Donna reminded him. "Bagging groceries at Food Town isn't going to make him rich," Bud mumbled. "But he needs a car and he's doing what you told him to do," she added. "But I thought we agreed to eat together one day a week... like a healthy family should," he said in frustration.

"Bud, let's face it. We're a long way from being a healthy family," Donna volleyed back. "And what do you mean by that?" he retorted quickly. "Well, a healthy family has a leader, someone who gives direction and is respected by the others," she remarked as she finished dishing out their food. "A leader? Why a leader?" asked Bud. "Because there are areas in our lives that we need to change," Donna responded. Bud sat silently staring at his food. This was the second marriage for them both. Six years ago they started together with great hopes and a ready-made family. Bud had a son and daughter living with him and Donna had never had kids and loved them both dearly.

"So exactly what areas do you think we need to change?" Bud snapped back. "Well, Bud, we've got health issues. Take your mom, for example. She's stuck in that awful nursing home. I go to see her every week but you never come. And you haven't spoken to her doctor in six months," Donna stated. "And exactly what am I supposed to talk to Dr. Franks about, pray tell?" shouted Bud. "Your mother is on nine different prescription drugs and disoriented half the time. That's what. She's your mom and you need to take responsibility for her at this point. You talk about doing something but nothing ever happens. They're your kids and she's your mom. I don't mind doing my share but you need to do yours," Donna stated pointedly.

"And what other health issues are bugging you?" Bud slammed back. "I'm worried about YOU. You're overweight, not sleeping, and we haven't had sex in months. And when did you have your last physical? You need to take responsibility for your health and well-being. And don't you dare tell me you're getting old because I know lots of men your age who are in great shape," she shouted before he could say a word.

"Let's get back to this leadership issue," said Bud hoping to change the subject. "The leadership issue is what I'm talking about. When family members are in pain, they need a leader to take care of them," Donna replied. "Pain, who's in pain?" snapped Bud. "Your son's in pain. He's failing in school! Do you think that feels good? He's in a class of 45, overcrowded to say the least. He needs you to help with his homework at night but do you notice? No, you sit in front of the TV at night sipping your beer. Chuck is 16 and he can't write a decent essay. And you're a professional writer for goodness sake! It's a joke. Bud needs basic writing skills if he's going to graduate from high school, not to mention go to college," Donna responded close to tears.

"Your daughter's in pain, too. Every time Babs asks you to do for something for her, you blow her off," Donna shouted. "Like when?" Bud demanded. "Like two weeks ago when she asked you to go to the homecoming game to watch her cheer, and you didn't. Or when she said she needed a parent to attend her debate last Saturday, and you told her you were too busy... and then you slept on the couch the whole time she was gone. Without a parent there, she had to sit out the debate and she arrived home in tears. Or when she asked you to proofread her term paper and you never "found time." A good leader makes time to teach and encourage, but you're in your own little world!" Donna said angrily as she finished clearing the plates from the table.

"So now that we're having this out, what else's on your chest?" Bud yelled. "Dah, how about our relationship?" Donna retorted. "We're time-starved and working ridiculous hours. We both know that, but when are you ever willing to sit down and talk? I'll tell you the answer. Only when I push you the way I'm doing now! And when do we make time to share plans and dreams; when was the last time you held me and said I love you? We're nothing more than roommates, rushing through the weeks and months of our lives and growing farther and farther apart!"

Bud was shocked. He knew what Donna had said was true, but it struck a bitter blow to his ego. He was working hard, very hard, to provide for this family. But he realized that Donna was too. He sat quietly thinking about each point she had made. Then without owning his behaviors or stepping up as a leader, he handed the problem back to her saying, "And what do you propose doing about this?"

"This is what you always do! You put the problem right back on me." Donna was furious, but she took a deep breath and began again. "We both love the kids and we can't screw this up. We just don't seem to be able to solve this problem ourselves. Are you willing to talk to an expert about this?" Donna asked. Shaken by the reality he was being forced to confront, he said "Yes." And Donna immediately looked up Susan's number and asked if she would be willing to talk through their situation with them. Susan listened carefully to the details each of them provided, made sure they knew they had been thoroughly heard, and began...

Sad to say, many parents don't see themselves as leaders

Today, many parents see themselves as overworked individuals who can barely make it through their day and need to rest when they finally get home. They forget they have family members who count on them not just to spend nights at home but to participate in their lives — to oversee their health, to teach them new skills, to help them become productive and competitive and create dreams of their own. Bottom line, they don't realize they are responsible for leading their children in all three gears.

Many parents are so mired down in making money and trying to please their bosses that they miss enjoying their children lives — listening to the events of the day, going to school plays, sports events, being there when there are successes as well as setbacks and failures. Then they suddenly "wake up" when their kids marry or move to their own homes or accept jobs in other cities or countries… and it's too late. The opportunity is gone.

I talk to far too many couples who lose each other along the way — making meals, returning phone calls, closing sales and gaining promotions. They work so long and so hard that their relationship dies before they reach the bottom of the pile of stuff on their desks or stop to notice that they are living separate lives.

Getting stuck in 2nd Gear — constantly racing and revving to do more-better-faster-cheaper, to climb higher on charts and graphs — will drive you over the edge unless you know how and when to shift up and down out of it. I remember sitting in the office of the CEO of one of America's largest companies on a day when a huge product roll-out was taking place. He was at the pinnacle of his career when the phone rang and, from across the room, I could hear his son yelling at the top of his lungs, "Dad, don't you dare promise me you'll make it to my game tonight. I don't believe you anymore. Your work's always first!" And that high-powered CEO laid his head down on his desk and sobbed bitterly. When he finally looked up, he stammered, "And, Susan, the worst part is my son is right. Over the years I have consistently sacrificed him for my job."

Relationships and families are like plants. We can't just start them and expect them to grow. Tending is our 1st Gear Leadership responsibility. Whenever we notice that people are in 1st Gear — our children, upset spouses or aging parents — we must make time to slow down and respond. When you were in 1st Gear, starting a new skill or reeling from a disappointment, injury or illness, what did you want? You probably wanted someone to stop and listen to your needs, to follow through with supportive actions and advice. That's what they want too, not all the time but when life and circumstances force them to gear down and depend on you.

Arriving at that product roll-out or awards conference will be lonely and disappointing if there is no one there to celebrate with us, if we have neglected our kids and families so much and so frequently that they no longer care about our success. And, even more dire, if they no longer want success themselves because we've taught them that success only means doing more-better-faster with no time left over for anything or anyone else... especially them.

And what about our dreams? Are we neglecting them too? Without dreams, our lives become humdrum and boring. Like rats on a wheel, we daily run the same circuit. It takes dreams to blast us out into new orbits and opportunities. And, it takes Co-dreamers—people who hold our dreams with us and even for us when we're disappointed or discouraged—to make those dreams powerful enough to attract us through obstacles and setbacks, disorientations and reorientations to realities enjoyed."

"Bud," Susan continued, "I don't think this crisis has much to do with your love for Donna and the kids. I think it has much more to do with your failure to grab "the gearshift of your life" and engage the Success or Leadership Gear that is needed in the moment. You've been relying on an automatic transmission that isn't working for you and your family. Most people don't realize they're in the driver's seat of their lives. They don't know they have gears and what each one is designed to do. A successful life doesn't just happen. It's something you must learn to drive. And it takes all three gears—used at the right time—to make the journey fulfilling and worthwhile. You need to shift manually.

With all that said, Bud, what do you need to do to change the way you listen to your family, the way you use your time and energy at home, the way you plan your days, nights and weekends?. And, what are your dreams, your personal destinations? What steps can you take in their direction today? By living our dreams, we show our families, friends and coworkers... in the most important way possible... that their dreams can come true too. We are leading by example wherever we are."

"Our children are watching us at home and at work. We are the ones who are teaching them about success. We are the ones who are responsible for building their confidence and enthusiasm, their hope and tenacity. We can teach them to succeed in two ways— we can tell them how to do it or we can do it ourselves."

Susan Ford Collins
Our Children Are Watching:
10 Skills for Leading the Next Generation to Success

Part Two

The 2nd Gear of Success and its essential companion—

the 2nd Gear of Leadership

Overview- 2nd Gear of Success—More-Better-Faster-Cheaper

Once you are consistently effective at your new job or skill...

- your leaders shift you into the more independent and more accountable 2nd Gear of Success; or if they fail to, you must shift yourself.
- in 2nd Gear the pace and expectations accelerate.
- the more work you do, the more work you're given.
- the more quality you produce, the more quality is expected.
- instead of sticking to Beginner's Rules, you begin taking shortcuts, dropping out steps and altering familiar methods.
- trying no longer counts; now you're expected not only to be effective but also efficient.
- you're expected to compete, to do more in less time at a higher quality with fewer people.
- the mantra of 2nd Gear is more-better-faster-cheaper.

In 2nd Gear you're working independently but...

- you are still dependent on your leaders.
- they're no longer there to give you immediate feedback.
- they're not always available to answer your questions.
- they're setting your goals and measurement standards.
- they're tracking your results.
- their charts and numbers signal when you're on track and off.
- their quotas and projections motivate or depress you.
- their bonuses and perks encourage or discourage you.
- your leaders regularly sit down with you to evaluate your productivity.
- they tell you what they expect from you next.

2nd Gear Word Signals: The following words let you know when you or someone else is operating in 2nd Gear...

more-better-faster, cheaper, produce, compete, win, lose, quantity, quality, goals, evaluations, promotions, bonuses, perks, timeframes, budgets, measures, deadlines, pressures, planning, projections, marketing, global completion, power, politics, demotions, firings, anger, spin control, investments, mortgages, credit cards, debt, retirement plans, wealth, stock prices, interest rates, points, profits, buyouts, layoffs, takeovers, stress, exhaustion, vacations, workouts, health issues, weight loss/gain, caffeine, ulcers, stress, tranquilizers, blood pressure, greed, corruption, depression, drugs, collapse, imprisonment, humiliation, death

These words give you a feel for what is most desirable—and most destructive—about 2nd Gear... depending on how sensitively you use it.

There is a time and place for everything. But 2nd Gear isn't right all the time. When do you need to shift into 1st Gear?

- whenever your momentum is disrupted.
- whenever there's major disruption or change.
- whenever new people, information, or skills are introduced.
- whenever your health and balance are compromised.
- whenever you need significantly higher levels of support.

And when do you need to gear up into 3rd?

- whenever you can't do any more, any better, any faster, any cheaper... using the methods that are in place.
- whenever you must breakthrough into creativity and innovation to achieve your outcome.

What should you watch for in 2nd Gear? A constant pressure...

- to say yes.
- to take on more, whether it's your job or not.
- to work longer and harder.
- to compromise your 1st Gear values and integrity.
- to spend more money and put more debt on your credit cards.
- to over-exercise, over-eat, to under-exercise, under-eat.
- to get out of balance at work and at home.
- to pay more attention to your boss's needs than your family's or your own.
- to stretch the truth, exaggerate, downplay... to lie.

- to break agreements with your kids to read a story, attend a sports events or help with a project.
- to cut short communications with your coworkers,
- to not know what matters to your spouse, what s/he is dreaming.
- to take an extra call or task at the last minute.
- to get home later than you said you would.
- to lose touch with family and friends.
- to lose touch with yourself.

Are you using 2nd Gear appropriately or are you overusing it?

- are you eating and exercising the way you know you should?
- how recently have you had a checkup or made time to relax? No, not some high-powered vacation but simply time to sit quietly and do the unthinkable... absolutely nothing.
- are you effective and efficient at your job?
- are you making the money you need and want?
- are you achieving goals on time?
- are you a top producer in your organization?
- can you gear down when circumstances require, when someone needs an answer to a question? Or someone wants to share an upcoming project and needs your input to proceed?
- are you willing to listen to dreams and thoroughly consider how important they are not just to success today, this quarter, appraisal, or evaluation, but to success in the future?
- are you living your values and honoring your integrity?
- are you making time for your dreams and your family's?
- are you so stuck in 2nd Gear that you can't slow down... even when you know you should?
- are you going so fast that you can't "see the forest from the trees"?
- are you exhausted, burned out and unenthusiastic?
- are you using foods or drugs to keep going or cover up pain?
- are you sacrificing your life, health, family and dreams for 2nd Gear results?
- have you seen companies fail because of 2nd Gear greed?
- have you seen people around you die from overusing 2nd Gear?

"We have a stick shift, not an automatic transmission. As we're thrown "curves" by technology and globalization, we need to disengage the clutch, downshift into the curve, and then give some gas (retooling via education, research and development, capital investment) before shifting back up into 2nd and accelerating out of the curve.

Globally, China, India and Eastern Europe are entering 2nd Gear while Western Europe and Japan are firmly stuck there, grinding away. The U.S. has led by excelling in 2nd Gear, and making enough forays into 3rd to reset the standards and redefine success. As more nations begin to excel in 2nd, the U.S. must spend more time in 3rd to maintain its lead.

The big question is whether enough of us will have the energy and creativity to spend increasingly more time in 3rd Gear. The second question is whether there will be enough of us left attending to the nuts and bolts."

Jack Scarborough, author of
The Origins of Cultural Differences and Their Impact on Management
Dean of the Business School at Barry University

The Call Center, a Modern-Day Sweatshop

It was Sunday night and Bunny was on the phone with her friend, Gloria, excitedly explaining how she'd just landed a job with Answer Direct. Gloria knew that Bunny had been receiving unemployment for some time and she was eager to hear how she had found this new job, "Well, the computers in the Unemployment Office display available jobs and this one looked interesting so I faxed them my resume and they called me the next day." "Wow, aren't you lucky. What's your salary?" Gloria asked. "$10.50 an hour," she responded. "And benefits?" Gloria asked. "No, are you kidding? Tomorrow is my first day. Call me tomorrow night and I'll tell you how it went."

Day One

"So, how did it go? And what did you do?" Gloria asked immediately. "Well, when we first got there we went to a 30-minute induction program," said Bunny. "Thirty minutes? What could you learn in 30 minutes?" Gloria asked. "Definitely not much. No one explained what we were supposed to do or why. They told us we would learn everything on the job. Then they introduced us to our supervisor and we went straight to work," Bunny said. "So what's your supervisor like?" Gloria wanted to know. "Who knows? He sits up in front of us. There are 40 of us in his division and from time to time he listens to our calls." "Is your job hard?" Gloria inquired. "No, we're handling customer calls for a large computer company. We listen to their questions and look up the answers on our computer screen and read them to our customers," "What happens if the answers aren't there?" Gloria asked. "They told us to cut them off politely," Bunny responded. "Knowing they will have to wait another 12 minutes in the queue, very few of them call back or write in to complain," she responded. "What a rip off!" exclaimed Gloria.

Day Two

"I'm exhausted," Bunny moaned on the phone. "Why? What happened? Gloria asked. "Our supervisor upped our quotas. Now instead of handling 20 incoming calls an hour, we have to handle 25. It just puts pressure on us to get off the phone faster." "That's shocking!" Gloria gasped. "I know. I'm a wreck tonight, I still don't know how to use to the equipment properly and there's no time to ask my Supervisor for help. It's one call after another from the moment I sit down." "And what are your offices like?" Gloria wanted to know. "Offices, are you kidding? We're in a giant warehouse with long strips of neon lights and no windows. There are 600 of us in tiny cubicles packed in like sardines. And you should see the washrooms, yuck!" moaned Bunny. "Sounds awful," Gloria screeched.

Day Three

"I'm not sure I can take this much longer," Bunny said in her their nightly call. "Why? What happened today?" Gloria asked. "Some guy went crazy in the parking lot and shot out his Supervisor's tires. The police came and arrested him," Bunny explained. "Oh that's awful," replied Gloria. "Tomorrow I'm being moved to a department that handles inbound calls for a large airline," Bunny said. "What will that entail?" asked Gloria. "Well, I'll have to give customers the prices for flying to destinations in the U.S. and issue electronic tickets. They gave me a 150 page manual to read tonight and I'll have a one hour training session in the morning," Bunny added. "Will they pay you more?" Gloria asked. "They said if I do a good job, I will go up to $11.50 an hour."

Day Four

"I'm working the airline account now," Bunny told Gloria on the phone that night. "How is it?" Gloria asked. "Well it's more complicated than I thought, but I have a great supervisor, Jackie, and she spent a lot of time helping me," Bunny replied. "A good supervisor makes a big difference." Gloria responded. "Yes, Jackie makes sure that I understand how to look up the fares and tests me to see if I'm doing it right. And she's always ready to answer my questions." Bunny added. "A bit different from the first one you had!" Gloria chimed in. "Yes, night and day," Bunny said with a yawn and a "good night."

Day Five

"Congratulations, you made it through the first week," Gloria exclaimed. "And how did it go today?" "Well, Jackie asked me to work nights starting next week," Bunny replied. "Nights? What time are nights?" Gloria asked. "6 pm to 2 am, with an hour for dinner," said Bunny. "Every night?" added Gloria. "Yes, every week night," affirmed Bunny." How do you feel about that?" asked Gloria. "Well, the way they put it, we don't have much choice." Bunny responded. "Gee, that's harsh." "Yes, it's a modern day sweat shop," Bunny added with a groan.

Day Fifteen

"Oh, I had a great idea today," Bunny said on their nightly call. "What was it?" asked Gloria. "Well I came up with a way to save a lot of time on incoming calls," Bunny replied. "How?" asked Gloria. "If we divide the incoming calls into six categories and each of us takes category, we wouldn't have to switch computer screens and it would save the company a ton of time," replied Bunny. "Did you tell your supervisor?" asked Gloria. "Yes, I told Jackie and she gave me a form to fill out and put in the suggestion box." Bunny answered. "Wow, you might get a big reward if they implement it," Gloria added enthusiastically.

Day Thirty

"Bunny, I was thinking about that idea you had a couple of weeks ago. Have you heard anything yet?" Gloria said on the phone. "No, I haven't heard anything from anyone. And that's typical," replied Bunny. "Gee, that's too bad. You were so pumped up," remembered Gloria. "That's the last time I'll offer them any of my suggestions," said Bunny. "I don't blame you," concluded Gloria as she said goodbye.

Day Forty-One

"Oh, Gloria, I screwed up today." Bunny said at the beginning on their nightly phone call. ""What in the world did you do?" Gloria asked. "I quoted a customer the wrong airfare. It was $65 dollars too low and I issued an electronic ticket," replied Bunny. "So what happened?" asked Gloria. "They gave me a warning, whatever that means. And told me that if I did it again I would be transferred to another department and taken back to $10.50," Bunny explained. "Do you have a boss you can talk to about this?" asked Gloria. "No, sad to say, my wonderful supervisor Jackie couldn't take it and left," Bunny said feeling quite defenseless.

Day Forty-Two

"You won't believe this, Gloria, they demoted me today. I've been moved and I'm back to $10.50 an hour," mumbled an upset Bunny on her nightly call to Gloria. "What are you doing now?" Gloria asked. "Well, there's a TV ad for a special kind of mattress. When people call for information. I take their name and address, phone number and best time to call back. It's a pressure cooker. They give you 45 seconds to get the details and the next call is already waiting," exclaimed Bunny. "Sounds awful," Gloria concluded.

Day Sixty

"Gloria, we went in this morning and some head-office guy told us they'd lost the mattress account and we were all being laid off." said Bunny. "What!" exclaimed Gloria "Can they do that? Aren't there labor laws that prevent that?" asked an indignant Gloria. "Well, when we came onboard we had to sign a form stating we were temps working on an hourly basis. So we have no rights," Bunny sighed. "Sounds like you're lucky to be out of there," Gloria added. "You bet. But I have to find something else right away. I need the money!" Bunny said in tears.

The working poor of America

Obviously Answer Direct wasn't using all three gears correctly. Their people were not adequately trained up and by the time they caught onto their job, they either left the company or had to start over in another department. Answer Direct was not productive and competitive. Their leaders were failing to acknowledge the cost of training and retraining these new people. All the unproductive days they have at the start. The mistakes poorly trained employees make and the damage they do to the customer base. Here's an essential truth: Employees in 1st Gear simply can't be expected to be efficient and productive.

Not only were Answer Direct's people not effective in 1st Gear or competitive in 2nd Gear, but their leaders were not able to shift to 3rd Gear to take advantage of the suggestions that Bunny and others made either. Instead of exploring creative ideas that would save their employees time and effort and make the company satisfying and profitable, they were pushing longer and harder on methods that were not working.

Answer Direct is 2nd Gear at its worst! It's certainly not a rewarding environment for potentially-capable employees to spend 10-12 hours a day.

The majority (60 percent) of creatives said that they have had "great ideas" in the last year but not enough time or support at work to achieve what they wanted.

Creativity Under Threat: No Time to Talk About It
September 25, 2013 PRNewswire New York

Mercury Investments: Safety and Trust

When Franklin Mercury started buying and selling rare stamps and coins in New York City in 1906, little did he know that 100 years later his small company would become the sixth largest investment firm in the U.S. Today Mercury Investments is a Wall Street powerhouse with 450 branch offices across the U.S., 27 offices overseas and 25 in-house mutual funds quoted on the Big Board.

When Mercury's Advertising VP, Darren Oats, met with their ad agency account executive, Sharon Platt, he stated firmly, "Two themes need to come through LOUD and CLEAR in next year's campaign, SAFETY and TRUST. Our focus groups came to the same conclusion," For Sharon, Mercury Investments was a $50 million dollar a year account and Sharon so she was quick to respond. "Darren, our present tag line, "no one looks after your investments better than we do" has done an outstanding job for you." "Yes but we need something fresh and positive for next year. The 'no one' bit struck a negative chord with our president," he explained. "How about a leadership theme?" Sharon asked. "Yes, we are leaders on Wall Street," Darren affirmed. All present agreed and they worked through the details until late afternoon.

Meanwhile at Mercury Investment's Chicago branch, Leslie Moser was pulling into the parking garage in her new BMW sports sedan. A single mom in her 40's with two teenage daughters and a mother to support, Leslie was grateful that she had been able to make a good living with Mercury. Headed toward her office, she glanced at the Dow futures on the board. "Up again!" When she sat down at her desk, she flipped through her client list. "What a game this is! This morning I earned money by selling 100 shares of Home Depot to client A and having Client B sell 100 shares of the same stock" Sharon thought as she estimated the commissions she had made in her head.

In New York, the marketing head Martin Baxter, Sr., who had MBA in finance from Harvard and was a legend in the industry at 43, was finalizing his report for the president. "It's a $7-trillion dollar pie and we need a bigger slice. I'm going to make it mandatory that our 2,300 financial advisers sell Mercury Mutual at every opportunity." He outlined his strategy in the report: 1- Sell "B" class shares instead of "A" because we make more profit and structure them so they're front- and back-end loaded (this means customers will have to pay a fee to get in and to get out). Make sure our mutual funds are non-transferable (this means customers who want to transfer them to another brokerage house will have to sell them and pay the back-end fee). 2- Increase administrative fees by 0.009 percent on all funds. This alone will result in another $16 million annually and only a few clients will notice the charge. 3- And finally, introduce an incentive over and above the current commission when advisers sell our ten poorest performing funds. Mark knew this was illegal but the industry was so loosely regulated that he never gave it a second thought. His recommendations had always sailed through the executive investment committee. "This will ensure my $5 million bonus at the end of the year," he thought with a competitive chuckle.

Back in Chicago, Leslie was talking to clients. She spoke in her "concerned voice" which had always proved successful with clients. She never used "I" but always "we." "We will sell 500 of GE and then put some of the proceeds into another 100 Carnival. Cruise sales are up," she stated with certainty. Her approach worked. Her clients trusted her and followed her recommendations. They all wanted someone to make them feel safe and certain. They wanted to feel she knew what she was talking about, since they didn't know themselves. The market was going up so everyone was happy, especially her branch manager whose million-dollar Christmas bonus depended on these commissions.

Then things began to change. First, there were rumors that the Securities and Exchange Commission (SEC) was investigating Mercury Investments. The head office neither admitted nor denied it, of course. Four weeks later, an article in *The Wall Street Journal* confirmed that the SEC was indeed investigating Mercury. The president issued a strong statement denying any wrongdoing and declaring that they would be exonerated. But the word spread like wild fire throughout the industry.

Leslie was worried, what should she tell the clients who had trusted and followed her recommendations for years? When they examined their monthly statements they would see that she had placed them in "B" class Mercury Mutual to earn the extra commission. They would notice that she had been churning their accounts and that most of the Mercury Mutual she had placed them in yielded low returns. Their own observations would confirm the SEC charges. The official line from head office was to admit nothing and say you have always acted in your client's best interests.

First a trickle, then two or three of her accounts a week started to move over to competitors. The golden goose had laid its last golden egg. Mercury Investments agreed to pay the SEC a $60-million fine. The following day, the president issued a statement, "We will act quickly to end this unfortunate chapter in our company's history. Our clients deserve nothing less."

Richard knew this story first hand because one of his associates, Jenny Major, was Leslie's client. "I trusted her," she told Richard, "And I blindly agreed with every recommendation she made." When I read the story in the newspapers, I asked my finance-expert cousin to look at my monthly Mercury statements. He told me that my years with Leslie had cost me thousands of dollars."

Leadership or Greedership? A 2nd Gear choice

J enny, you were in 1st Gear, and you were following a leader who wasn't worthy of your trust. You thought you were doing the right thing, but the company and its executives were manipulating the game. They were motivated by profits, not ethics and fair play."

"How could my broker have done this to me?" That's a question far too many investors have been asking during the last few years. When you are in 1st Gear, you're depending on a leader to make decisions for you. Therefore you must select the most reputable expert you can find. In 1st Gear you're an easy target for the unscrupulous and unethical. You are easily manipulated and snookered because you simply don't know.

Leadership or Greedership? This is the question. When industries and companies overuse 2nd Gear, they forget about the trust their 1st Gear customers place in them. They are far more concerned about profits and bonuses than the good-faith agreement they have with the public. We need Three-Gear Leaders today—leaders who are able to keep their balance in all three Gears: leaders who honor their 1st Gear responsibilities to keep their client's money safe and secure, to tell the truth and play by fair rules; leaders who remember their 2nd Gear responsibilities to make the investment profitable for their client and only take their fair share; and leaders who respect their 3rd Gear responsibilities to know when they are pushing the limits of 2nd Gear and they need to create new ways of making returns that still meet their standards of honesty and integrity.

We live in a society that is overusing 2nd Gear, pushing longer and harder to make and spend money. We are teaching our kids to overuse 2nd Gear too, winking at cheating and unfairness, praising results at the cost of their health and integrity, making grades and scores more important than their creativity. It's time to update our ideas about success and leadership.

What is success? Let's go back to our original question. Is it being right and following the rules? Is it making money and accumulating possessions? Is it being creative and innovative? No, to thrive, it must be a balance of all three. And what is leadership? Leadership is being able to guide those around us to succeed in all three gears too.

"If you seek to lead, invest at least 50% of your time in leading yourself—your own purpose, ethics, principles, motivation, conduct. Invest at least 20% leading those with authority over you and 15% leading your peers."

Dee Hock, Founder and CEO Emeritus
Visa

Could Suzi Escape The Success Trap?

Suzi Day was bright—she had graduated from Columbia with honors in journalism and spent the next 20 years freelance writing from home. Her specialty was articles, book reviews and in-depth profiles for women's magazines. She had developed a special talent for pursuing, in the nicest way, hard-to-reach celebrities till they relented and agreed to an interview.

When her 15-year marriage ended in divorce, she continued writing with even more determination. Money was a much higher priority now that their younger son, David, had moved in with her. Starting a new household and paying all the bills was a struggle, but she was able to keep up until the economy took a dip and her freelance work evaporated. Suzi spent hours each day searching the web, looking for ideas she could turn into stories to sell. But the approach that had worked so well for her in the past had come to an abrupt stop. Apart from an occasional book review or interview, she found it impossible to sell freelance articles any more.

What to do? She had to have money and, having always worked for herself, she was hesitant to work full-time for someone else. It was Thanksgiving and she joined her family for their annual get together. Her older brother, Phil, a successful banker, listened to the ins and outs of her plight and concluded, "Suzi, you're a smart cookie. You just need to recreate yourself." "Yeah, but how?" asked Suzi. "Start thinking about the writing jobs you could do from home—not just for publications—and go after them," he advised. "You make it sound so easy," she replied. "I think it will be. Use your brains and you'll surprise yourself," he said confidently.

Returning home, Suzi thought about how she could use her skills. "I'll have to think outside the box," she told herself and a few nights later, while surfing the web, she spotted an ad which read, "Can you write? Need part time work? Contact us." A market research firm in New York City was advertising for writers. She applied by email and was asked to submit a sample of her work that same afternoon.

To be considered, Suzi would have to listen to hours of audio tapes from focus groups and write a 30-page report with conclusions. Suzi was psyched. She dropped everything and spent three days listening and writing, not knowing whether there would be a payoff or not. After reading her sample report, the president of the company, Nancy Witt, called to say she was delighted with what Suzi had produced and asked her to fly to New York for some specialized training. What a break! Suzi was thrilled.

A week later Suzi was in the New York offices of Market Research America attending one-day training on moderating focus groups. While there, she and Nancy started talking about the agency's challenge of recruiting high-quality respondents. The agency was particularly interested in improving the quality of patients and physicians they found for their many pharmaceutical company clients. Suzi realized she had the skills required so she proposed taking over that responsibility. To her delight, Market Research America said, "Yes!" Suzi had managed to create a job that paid well and offered her the opportunity to learn and grow professionally.

Within no time at all, Suzi was their star. She was able to put together difficult groups like busy neurosurgeons and cardiac surgeons. Using her Internet skills, she was able to track down patients with rare diseases and bring them together for telephone focus groups. When Suzi completed her second project, Nancy sent a bouquet of long-stemmed roses with a thank you note and a $500 bonus.

As the weeks passed, Suzi realized Nancy was the most demanding boss she had ever had. Nancy's deadlines were impossible and Suzi soon found herself working days, nights and weekends. If she wasn't making calls to recruit respondents, she was typing up reports. When one job ended, another began. She barely had time to deposit her checks.

But she couldn't slow down because she needed the money. She began losing weight and rescheduling get-togethers with her friends. She started ordering in fast foods and stopped working out. Dirty clothes were piled up in her bedroom chair. Her house was a wreck, and most distressing of all, her son was constantly upset because there was nothing in the refrigerator to eat. Yes, she was making money but....

Then one day Suzi missed a deadline and Nancy was on the phone raving, shouting and screaming. Suzi was stunned. After having worked so hard and producing such outstanding results, she couldn't believe this was how she was being treated. But what would happen if she let Nancy down again and she stopped feeding her business? She would just have to work harder. So she started drinking black coffee to keep her awake late into the night, and then she wangled some pills to keep her alert during the day. It was a race against the clock. The more-better-faster work she did, the more Nancy sent... along with an occasional bonus and flowers.

One weekend after Suzi completed a demanding project and had a couple of days free, she decided to speed-read four books that had been sitting on her desk. One of those books was *The Joy of Success, 10 Essential Skills for Getting the Success You Want*. As she skimmed the pages, she saw her life unfold in front of her eyes. She was stuck in 2nd Gear and unable to gear down into1st or up into 3rd. Suzi knew she was caught in The Success Trap. When she saw my website on the jacket of the book she contacted me about her dilemma.

Here's how I responded.

Dear Suzi, you're not alone

Suzi, you're not alone. Millions of top producers are caught in The Success Trap, working longer and harder but never getting one iota closer to the lives they desire. Let's take a few minutes to get a glimpse of The Big Picture of Success. As kids, we succeeded by pleasing other people... our parents and teachers. We learned to do what they wanted us to do, the way they wanted us to do it. We felt successful when they smiled or rewarded us. Remember those stars and special privileges and treats and how much they meant to us? When we first went to work, success meant the same thing — doing what our boss wanted us to do the way he or she wanted it done. Yes, 1st Gear is essential for learning and startup. BUT, then the training is over and we start working on our own. We're handed deadlines and expected to meet them.

In 2nd Gear, we feel independent, but we aren't, Suzi, as you are finding out. We are still dependent on our boss's standards and timeframes, on getting the next piece of work, promotion or raise. To get more we have to do more and more and more, and sooner or later, if we remain in 2nd Gear, we end up where you are. HELP! You've done about as much more-better-faster as you can, and still survive.

Suzi, you have a choice. You can keep pushing in 2nd until something stops you — your health, your son wanting to go live with his dad, or, God forbid, you're so strung out that you make a huge mistake or have a life-threatening accident.

Or, you can shift into 3rd Gear and take a fresh look. What do you really want? Is it just money, or does it involve quality of life and enjoyment of dreams? Obviously you haven't had much time to dream lately but, Suzi, you must. Dreams are what make your life worth living. Dreams are what make you wake up in the morning eager and excited, the way your son does when he knows he's going to the circus.

When you're stuck in 2nd Gear, all you think of is money and pleasing your boss. But the real joy of success is far more subtle and enticing. Remember when you recreated yourself last time and you just happened to find that ad and respond? You sensed an opportunity and created a job that fit your skills and interests. Well, it's time to do that again. But this time you know more about what you want... and you don't want. This time you have connections with pharmaceutical firms who know your work even though they don't know you. What's happened in the marketplace? What new opportunities are out there?

Suzi, be sure to ask yourself: "What are my needs versus my wants?" Corporate America sells what *they* want you to buy, but it's up to you to assess the truth of their marketing claims. Do *you* really need all the appliances and gadgets they want you to have? Do *you* really need a new car every three years? Do *you* want to live up to Corporate America's expectations… or your own? Take charge of your life and set a new course. Ask yourself the questions you've been too numb to ask: Do I really want to live how and where I am living? Do I really need to pay for this lifestyle? And what is it costing me… besides the money?

"73% of respondents said they would be willing to move their careers to the back seat for their families."

2003 Spherion Emerging Workforce Study

Overview: 2nd Gear of Leadership— Measure, Evaluate, Reward, Stay Available

What sort of leadership do your followers need in 2nd Gear?

- spell out specific details and timeframes for their job.
- specify precisely what you will be measuring and how.
- provide timely feedback, charts and graphs.
- sit down for face to face to appraisals on a regular basis, be available in between.
- offer incentives for improving performance… perks, bonuses, promotions and raises.
- give more freedom as they assume more responsibility, as results improve.
- expect them to experiment, drop out steps and question procedures.
- monitor effectiveness and efficiency of their short cuts.
- allow them to develop more efficient approaches unless interface with other jobs and departments would be compromised, unless safety would be threatened or integrity breached.
- encourage them to discuss their ideas with you so they can integrate your experience, expertise and knowledge.
- listen carefully to their suggestions for product, process and system improvements.
- gear them back to 1st Gear with them if they make serious errors or production drops below standards.

What do you need to do at this point in the success process? You need to...

- spell out corrective actions they need to take
- reaffirm 1st rules and requirements
- retrain and refocus on skills, information, mission and integrity.
- acknowledge progress as they are relearning
- continue to rebuild their self-confidence.
- Gear back to 2nd Gear when they're ready

As a 2nd Gear Leader you must decide...

- what rewards do you currently have in place?
- are you rewarding 2nd Gear more-better-faster-cheaper behaviors disproportionately?
- are you excessively bonusing, perking and promoting individuals overusing 2nd Gear? Are you committed to Leadership or Greedership?

- will these rewards result in errors, stress, burnout, and breaches of integrity and mission?
- are you rewarding people for continuing to use the same methods, systems and equipment while your competitors are creating, innovating, and moving ahead?
- what will overusing 2nd Gear cost you in the long run?
- are you also rewarding 1st Gear successes—learning new programs, information, and skills that will be needed to continue succeeding and leading?
- are you also rewarding 3rd Gear successes—their new ideas and approaches?
- did you know that your evaluation and reward systems will determine where people invest their time and energy, and where they don't?
- are you rewarding staying true to values, honesty, integrity and cooperation?
- are you rewarding individuals and teams who are productive and competitive?
- are you rewarding individuals who are devising improved methods and systems?
- are you rewarding individuals who are generating new ideas and insights?
- are you rewarding individuals whose new ideas could take you, your organization and society to the next level?

- are you rewarding individuals and teams for making time to develop and sell their ideas to you and others in-house… instead of selling them to a competitor?

2nd Gear Word Signals: The following words let you know when you or someone else is operating in 2nd Gear…

more-better-faster, cheaper, produce, compete, win, lose, quantity, quality, goals, evaluations, promotions, bonuses, perks, timeframes, budgets, measures, deadlines, pressures, planning, projections, marketing, global completion, power, politics, demotions, firings, anger, spin control, investments, mortgages, credit cards, debt, retirement plans, wealth, stock prices, interest rates, points, profits, buyouts, layoffs, takeovers, stress, exhaustion, vacations, workouts, health issues, weight loss/gain, caffeine, ulcers, stress, tranquilizers, blood pressure, greed, corruption, depression, drugs, collapse, imprisonment, humiliation, death

These words give you a feel for what is most desirable—and most destructive—about 2nd Gear… depending on how sensitively you use it.

Be on the lookout for individuals who are shifting up into 3rd Gear creativity:

- keep channels of communication open; you never know who and when they will breakthrough.
- let go of your preconceived ideas about who is creative and what is impossible.
- gear up into the 3rd Gear of Leadership with them.
- take time to visualize and thoroughly understand what they are suggesting.
- evaluate the costs and benefits of what they are proposing.
- stay out of competition. Co-dream and Co-operate with them.
- support their process and steer them past needless 1st and 2nd Gear barriers.
- guide them to the expertise they will need… wherever where it is.
- create an environment of cooperation and sharing, of Co-dreaming and collaborating.
- support them in having the time and resources they will need.
- sanction unofficial work until it can become official.
- offload as much non-essential work as possible.
- share their vision or dream with key people in your organization to gain buy-in.

- hold their dream for them when work pressures and obstacles overwhelm them.
- remember, every idea was impossible until someone made it possible.

"Through exceptional learning and performance,
we create a world that works better."

**Mission of The American Society
for Training and Development**

Moving Back Home, the 2nd Gear Squeeze

Parked in the tree-lined driveway of her childhood home, Sandy Elliot gazed through the windshield of her eight year old SUV. Turning the engine off, she slumped behind the wheel remembering when she was 18 and she left home for college. Now at 38, she was moving back in again. How did this happen?

Sandy had a great start, earning her Bachelor's in Social Work at twenty two and marrying Morris at twenty four. During their early years together, Morris taught in a local school and Sandy worked for Social Services. They weren't earning a fortune (her salary was $24,000 and his was $36,000), but they were happy and dreaming of an exciting future. After 15 years, they had managed to save $60,000 for a home.

The Stock Market Crash of 2008 wiped out their hopes for home ownership. When the dust settled, their nest egg had shrunk by 30%. Only $40,000 was left, the same amount Sandy had earned her first two years out of college. They looked for ways to save money and cut out everything they could without eliminating necessities. Finally in desperation, Morris suggested to Sandy that she ask her mom Norah if they could move in with her. They could save the $1500 a month in rent they were paying, and in exchange, they could help Norah with her medical expenses. It looked like a win-win. Norah was thrilled. Her husband had died of a heart attack in his early 60's and left her in the house alone. Now in her 80's, she was thinking of selling it and moving to a retirement community. With Sandy and Morris there, she could enjoy their company and their help.

Morris loved teaching and knew it was his calling. But lately he had been complaining a lot. There was the classroom size—45 per class made it impossible for him to do his job to his standards. There were lots of discipline problems. The kids in his school didn't respond to authority. They took the law into their hands and did whatever they pleased. In some classes, he had 25 or more students who refused to speak English and constantly chatted among themselves in their native tongues. There was the constant pressure from the Principal to keep their grades up. He insisted Morris give a specific number of A's and B's even though the quality of work deserved D's or F's in Morris's mind. By Friday afternoon, he was exhausted and he wanted to drink beer and stare mindlessly at sports on TV.

On top of that they were time-starved. Monday through Friday, sunrise to sundown, was one frantic rush. Sandy spent evenings reading and replying to 60 plus emails from work. Morris ground through endless paperwork now required of the teaching staff. God knows what people with kids do, Sandy mused.

But, in fact, she did know. In her job she dealt with overworked parents and their children every day. Her daily case load was overwhelming and, despite her best efforts, she was frequently two to three weeks behind even on urgent issues—like kids driving without licenses and wrecking their parent's cars, the ever-present drug problems and parent meetings with police, and the heart-to-heart talks about teenage pregnancies and what to do with their kids' kids.

The first few weeks back home were a relief. But little by little new pressures arose. They didn't realize how "old school" Sandy's mom had grown. For her, life was about right and wrong, black and white, good and bad. They couldn't have the TV on too loud. They had to turn off the lights whenever they left the room, even for a few minutes. They had to eat together even though their lives ran on different schedules. Sandy and Morris were feeling frustrated and restricted. It was like childhood again, but it was Norah's house and they weren't paying rent.

They used to eat out two or three times a week, but now only on Saturdays. They used to take two week vacations to Europe and South America, but now only a four-day Bahamas cruise in a lower deck cabin. They were paying outrageous interest charges on credit card balances they ran up before deciding they had to abandon their own home. They spent hours each week at the kitchen table trying to figure out what to do. Then, there was the cost of Norah's medications they agreed to pay instead of rent. Sure, she was on Medicare, but they hadn't realized that Medicare didn't cover the whole cost of her prescriptions. Or all of them.

All these pressures were causing friction between them too. They were arguing over silly things. Leisure time... what was that? They were facing information overload from their jobs and had no time to read bestselling novels they once enjoyed. Subscriptions to magazines and newspapers they used to savor over coffee were long gone. So were their stimulating and heated debates over social issues. Even their intimacy had suffered. They were too tired at the end of a long week for anything but sleep.

Oh yes, in the good old days Morris had long school vacations to rest up or visit his family in Maine. But now school holidays were spent working in the paint department at Home Depot. Morris is making extra cash for that dream house that seems to keep slipping farther and farther away as home prices continue to soar.

They can't afford to serve

We all know people who want to continue teaching, doing social work, nursing, law enforcement or helping kids and mothers eat a healthy diet. But it is becoming more and more difficult to "afford" to do these jobs. Many talented, dedicated social service providers are being forced to leave their jobs.

The Elliots are a childless couple. How much pressure do parents who have children feel as they struggle to feed, clothe, educate and provide healthcare for them? Will the fabric of their relationships and families continue to hold together? Or will it tear apart and cost our society even more.

What will happen if we allow our current obsession with 2nd Gear to squeeze out these workers who serve our 1st Gear needs... our needs for safety, health and education? When 1st Gear needs go unmet, we are unable to fulfill our 2nd and 3rd Gear responsibilities effectively. Ask any manager what happens to their employees' productivity when their marriages are in trouble, their children are ill or injured, their homes are damaged in a storm or fire. Our way of life is being challenged in front of our eyes and we can't even see it!

Our society needs skilled, compassionate people to lead our next generation to success, to help our children cope with the challenges they face... in homes with overworked parents, in overcrowded classrooms, in communities whose social service budgets have been deeply cut. We need people to prepare our children to assume the personal responsibility that will be needed to develop and redevelop their careers in tomorrow's workplace.

What will happen if we allow our current obsession with 2nd Gear to squeeze out the 3rd Gear creativity that we will be needed to move ahead as a society? What insights and middle-of-the-night realizations will be ignored and go unexplored? What old methods and outmoded structures will hold us back as a result? By forcing these individuals to give up their jobs, are we inadvertently destroying the quality of our lives as well?

And what impact will our current obsession with 2nd Gear have on our children? What decisions will kids who constantly see their parents struggling in 2nd Gear make about success... whether they want it or not? Are we pulling our kids into The 2nd Gear Squeeze along with us? Pressing them to compete and win, to participate in so many activities they don't have time to rest and relax, scheduling them so heavily that they don't have time to appreciate nature or play alone in the yard, they don't have time to exercise and stay in shape. Sound familiar?

What is success? That all depends. Success in 1st Gear is being able to care for our health, safety, security, environment and values. Success in 2nd Gear is being productive and competitive enough to provide for ourselves, our families and our dreams. Success in 3rd Gear is making our unique 1contribution, bringing forth ideas, products and fruitful new ways of living and moving our society ahead. We urgently need to teach our leaders at home, at work and in our communities... parents, teachers, governmental and business leaders... when each Success and Leadership Gear is needed and how to shift in and out smoothly.

We saw lots of shifting errors in this story. Sandy and Morris were being pushed harder and harder in 2nd Gear at work, but they weren't being given 2nd Gear salaries, perks and bonuses for assuming these responsibilities. This approach won't work any better here than it did at Jobs and Benefits, the Call Center or Pharmco. The same result will occur: the best people will leave and the ones who remain will be demoralized and unproductive. How about the mis-gear-match between Morris, Sandy and her mom? Norah was in 1st Gear worrying about security and health while Sandy and Morris had next to no time for 1st Gear for themselves. Will adult children who move back home be gear-flexible enough to shift into 1st without becoming irritable or unloving? Can they appreciate their parents' 1st Gear needs and fears? Or will they ship their parents away to nursing homes where they will be "taken care of" by strangers… out of sight, mind and heart?

"Two million teachers are needed. But half will quit
in the first five years."

Failing Grades, CNN Moneyline

"People who care for adult family members or friends fulfill an important role not only for the people they assist, but for society as a whole. While this care is unpaid, its value has been estimated at 257 billion dollars annually."

AARP

New York to Mumbai, a Nanosecond Away

Early one winter morning, Charles Merryweather charged down the stairs of the Larchmont train station. A cold wind struck his face as he bought a *New York Times* to read on his 30-minute commute into New York City. The platform was crowded for the 7:46 Express. At Grand Central, he grabbed coffee and a bagel and headed for his office at one the world's largest financial firms.

As a Financial Analyst, he knew another long week of sifting through data, running programs and turning out lengthy reports loomed ahead. But where else could he earn $200,000 a year, even though that wasn't a lot of money when he thought about what he took home and what he paid in expenses?

He and his wife, Wendy, had just moved to a 40-year-old, two-bedroom house in Larchmont. They were renting a Manhattan loft for $2,800 a month but when they found out they were expecting their first child, they decided to buy. They didn't get a lot of house for a half million dollars, but an equivalent apartment in Manhattan would have been $950,000... and way out of their range. Larchmont was an easy train ride into the city and his pharmacist wife landed a job in nearby New Rochelle.

That same Monday in Mumbai (formerly Bombay) it was hot and humid. India has a special fragrance, thought Sunny Dalal as he made his way through the crowded streets. Stopping to buy a cup of steamy, sweet milky tea and The India Express, he immediately turned to the sports page. "Finally, the Indians performed when it mattered. They destroyed the New Zealanders and won by a whopping 145 runs. Thank goodness we are winning at cricket," he thought, as he entered his company's building and made his way to his desk. Turning on his computer, he saw several emails including one from Charles Merryweather in the New York office.

His life in Mumbai was much simpler than his New York counterpart's. As a senior accountant with a CA (Charted Accountant) degree, he was a Financial Analyst too, but only making $14,000 a year. He was constantly frustrated by the endless demands his company made for higher and higher productivity with little or no reward. He realized he was being treated unfairly but, with so many CA's seeking work, he decided to grin and bear it. Sunny lived with his wife Coomi in a small one-room flat that was walking distance from his office. His parents had left him the flat and it was his prize possession.

Back in New York, Charles's boss, Doug Graham, was in a monthly strategic planning session on the 55th floor of their corporate headquarters overlooking Central Park. It was a gut-wrenching, closed-door affair with seven VP's present. "Yes, we know times are tough; investors have been scared away; the IPO business has virtually dried up, and we've got to cut costs. Your bonuses will depend on it," Chairman Bruce Crabtree threatened. Doug mumbled to himself, "This is a preamble to job-cutting. I can feel it coming." "You fat bastard," he thought, looking through his bifocals at Chairman Crabtree's stomach. Next the corporate accountant Jack Williams took the floor, "I guess this comes as no surprise but we have to reduce payroll. It's not so much the salaries but the additional 23% in the benefit package that's killing us," he continued.

Then Crabtree spoke without looking up from the papers he was fumbling, "Sooooo, Doug, you'll have to reduce your payroll by $450,000 next year." "And how the hell do I do that with the same work load or greater?" Doug volleyed back. There was a long silent pause and then Jack spoke up, "Well, if we replaced four of your Financial Analysts with four Financial Analysts in our Mumbai office, we could save $450,000 next year." Then the Chairman jumped in, "Exactly! That analysis can be done anywhere in the world. With today's technology, our Mumbai office is only a nanosecond away."

Doug stared down at his reflection in the shiny glass-top table and saw a disheartened face. He was stunned but not shocked. He knew their United Kingdom office was sending most of their analysis to India and so were their competitors. Would he or one of his people be next? Then he chuckled to himself, "A stone's throw away, ha! With today's technology, Mumbai's a nanosecond away."

Later that week, Doug told Charles he was sending him to India for four weeks to help their new hires understand how global operations worked. "Four weeks? I can give them an overview in two days." Doug's tone changed suddenly, "Listen Charles, they asked for four weeks so four weeks it is. Look at it this way; you'll stay in a great hotel and see the sights."

"Hey Doug, you've got to level with me. Is my job going overseas?" Charles queried as he glanced outside at the endless skyscrapers that dotted the Manhattan skyline and then back at Doug. "It looks that way, Charles. It sure does. Go over there, do a good job and I'll get you a three-month severance package, I swear."

Later that night, Charles broke the news to Wendy. "My work is done on a computer so it can be sent anywhere in the world. If I refuse to go to Mumbai, I won't get a severance package. But if I go, that $65,000 or so will give me time to find something else." Wendy was shocked," It's not fair," she sobbed bitterly. "Look at how loyal you've been and how hard you've worked. And this is how they reward you?" "My dear Wendy, fair has no meaning in the business world today. Besides, you know when one door closes another one opens. Let's wait and see…"

A few nights later as Charles headed home on the 7:16 Express, he was starring mindlessly at a vapor trail a plane approaching Kennedy was leaving in the sky when a future scene popped into mind. He was commuting between the U.S. and Mumbai and had his own research firm. He was outsourcing for the smaller New York financial houses that needed quality research but couldn't afford fulltime staff. Using his computer and modem, he was checking the Indian analyses and tweaking them for his U.S. consumers.

Wow, what an opportunity he'd been handed: $65,000 startup capital plus a four-week, all expense-paid, trip to Mumbai to get it going! No one knew better than Charles what had to be done and what services would sell in the U.S. All he needed was a partner in India and they could out do the giant Wall Street firms with their fat executive salaries and huge overheads.

That night he shared his vision with Wendy, and she could see it too. "But, Charles, you will have to move out of your comfort zone to make this happen," she added. He realized he would but, with his new dream in mind, energy was boiling up inside him.

Three weeks later, Charles was having lunch with his Indian counterpart, Sunny Dalal, in a small neighborhood restaurant in downtown Mumbai. They were so much alike in their thinking yet so far apart in their cultures and locations. Nevertheless there was a bond, and Charles began sharing his dream company. He spelled it out in graphic detail, what it looked like, sounded like and felt like right down to how the letterhead would feel in his hands. Soon Sunny stepped into Charles's dream and started adding details, offering expert advice and providing the names of people in Mumbai they should approach, figuring out timelines and even where they should open bank accounts. Charles had been scribbling notes on a paper napkin and he had no place left to write. It was exciting and both men's minds were overflowing with ideas. They were creating and co-creating and, in that moment, they both knew it would all come to pass. That is the Creative Certainty that allows us to bring dreams into realities and to move our lives and society ahead day by day. That was the quality that allowed them to succeed when others around them failed.

Merryweather, Dalal and Associates was founded that day in a Mumbai restaurant. Today MDA has fourteen full-time partners in India and three in New York. Their work is so good that Charles's old firm is a customer… much to Chairman Bruce Crabtree's chagrin.

"We'll see the entry of low-cost knowledge laborers doing to Wall Street what low-cost manufacturing laborers did to Main Street"

**Richard D'Aveni, Professor of Strategic Management
Tuck School of Business, Dartmouth College**

It takes all three Success Gears to create the future you dream

Here's a guy who saw the handwriting on the wall. His job was rapidly moving overseas and that four-week trip was scheduled so he could train his Indian replacements. Yet he turned lemons into lemonade.

One of the most important success skills is the ability to act on a hunch. Whether it was Post-It Notes or Teflon, the new idea popped up instantaneously and unexpectedly. The difference between the guys who go to the next level, and the ones who are left behind, is their ability to recognize that dream and nurture it all the way to a reality — a new product, business, or system.

In that jet-stream flash Charles had on the train, he realized that he and Sunny were doing the same job, in the same company, in different economies. The difference in the price structures of those economies would give them the profit edge that would allow their business to succeed. Instead of looking for another job in corporate America — something most people would have automatically done — Charles seized the opportunity to go to Mumbai and find an Indian analyst with whom he could team up. Charles and Dalal realized that if the marketplace was going global, they could go too.

If our partners at work and at home are going to support us through all the ups and downs, they will need to understand the Three Gears of Success and Leadership. Simply saying "How could they do this?" Or, "This isn't fair," won't be enough. Our spouses and partners will have to be able to use all three gears to steer us, our companies, families and careers. They will have to become Co-dreamers, encouraging us to take steps forward rather than retreat to familiar ways that no longer work. Those who can dream, and hold dreams, will move ahead in new directions and those who tenaciously try to move back into "how it used to be" or "how it always worked before" will be left behind… wishing nothing had changed. But it has.

Most people don't know what it takes to bring an idea into reality. It's not like fast food or 30-minute TV shows; it's a step-by-step, day-by-day process of discovery… and tenaciously holding onto your dream. This is the new reality… like it or not. Make sure you are ready to operate in all Three Success and Leadership Gears so the journey will be satisfying and the result fulfilling to all involved.

"We provide our people with all the tools they need to navigate where, when and how they work, and we trust that they will find the flexibility that helps both them and the firm succeed."

Maryella M. Gockel, Flexibility Strategy Leader
Ernst and Young

From Charity Auction to Secure Future

It was the first of the month and Marge and Harry were sitting at the dining room table pouring over their pile of bills. Yes, they could easily pay them online, but bill paying was a ritual they had performed together for forty years. It was their opportunity to regularly look at where they were financially and where they wanted to be.

Harry had worked in construction and always earned good money — good enough to allow Marge to stay home and raise their four kids. They had paid their bills on time and never accumulated debt except for their mortgage which was finally paid off. They hoped their $60,000 in savings, in addition to Harry's salary, would be enough. But two years ago Harry developed rheumatoid arthritis in both hands and could no longer work in construction. The only position he could find was as a $10-an-hour security guard at a local mall. So in their early sixties, they were sharing something new …a financial crisis.

"We're spending more than we're earning since you left your job. In fact, we're slipping behind $1500 a month," Marge said pointing to the numbers she had jotted down. "What can we cut?" Harry asked. "Well, the truth is, not much. Our biggest expense is our HMO, $700 a month, and your prescriptions add an extra $400. But we can't do without those," she added supportively. "With 4 1/2 years till Social Security kicks in, we'll need an extra $20,000 just to get by," Marge lamented. Marge and Harry are in the Baby Boom Squeeze millions of their fellow generation soon will be facing. They've had many good years but they haven't saved enough to retire in today's far more expensive world.

That night after dinner, Marge saw an ad in the local paper: Start Your Own Business. 8 Sessions for $50. "Aha! I think that's it!" Marge shouted out as she handed the paper to Harry. The course was at a nearby college so she immediately enrolled.

The first thing Marge's professor, Shirley Ball, asked her class to do was list their skills. "If you can drive a car, write that down. If you can paint, grow flowers, cook, use a computer or manage finances, put it down," she instructed. "These basic skills can be used in numerous businesses, "she said. "If you can drive a car, you can start your own limousine service. If you can use a computer, you can start a resume service." Shirley's ideas had Marge's brain working overtime. Soon she was feeling more optimistic about their future.

At the second class, Shirley asked them to list their hobbies, interests and activities. Marge included volunteering at her local church. On reviewing Marge's answers, Shirley pushed for more detail. "What sort of volunteer work have you done there, Marge?" "Once a year I make gift baskets for our charity auction. They sell quite well!" Marge said with a proud smile. "How much do you sell them for?" Shirley inquired. "Between $30 and $40," Marge responded quickly. "And what's in them for that price?" Shirley wanted to know. "Homemade cakes, jams and chocolates. I make them myself," beamed Marge. "Well then, that's your business!" Shirley shouted. "Next week we'll start working on your business plan."

At the end of eight weeks, Marge had a well-developed plan for Baskets to Your Door, Inc. She had prelived it dozens of times with her classmates and taken a reluctant Harry through all the details. "I have most of the skills I'll need. And, Harry, you're free a lot. You could shop for me some mornings and deliver baskets some afternoons." "And when will I sleep?" he replied with a wink. "At our age, how much sleep do you need?" Marge volleyed back and continued uninterrupted. "And where we lack skills, we'll hire experts. We'll need a good accountant to keep track of our profits and expenses," Marge added, sounding like a new CEO.

"Our plan calls for $12,000 startup capital," Marge reminded him. "That much?" a stunned Harry asked. "Well, my professor says we'll need that amount if we're going to produce a classy brochure, build a slick website and deliver sample baskets to local merchants to get them behind us. I'll get a business loan."

At the bank, Marge slammed head on into an unanticipated roadblock. The bank manager they'd done business with for fifteen years turned her loan application down. Marge had no prior business experience and he considered her "a high risk with a good idea."

Marge was undaunted, and her classmates cheered her on. "Harry, then we'll have to use our savings. If we don't invest in ourselves, that money will soon be gone anyway," Marge insisted. But Harry was nervous. Instead of seeing images of money coming in, he saw their savings going up in smoke. Harry knew what Marge was capable of, even if the bank didn't! Her managerial abilities were well-proven. She had raised four kids and managed them skillfully each step of the way to high-paying careers. The more Harry thought about it, the better he felt. After sleeping on it overnight, with a broad smile he agreed.

The first six months of Baskets to Your Door were harder than anyone had imagined. It was one thing to design a marketing plan but quite another to implement it. "Hard work never killed anyone," Marge chided Harry. He hoped he would survive startup, but there was no turning back now!

Then in the fifth month, Marge's efforts paid off. A local merchant who received a sample basket introduced Marge to the purchasing agent for a cruise line who gave her a trial order for 25 gift baskets. The cruise ship guests were thrilled and he immediately ordered 85 each Saturday. With this success under her belt, Marge sent baskets to six other cruise ships and soon found herself with a standing order for 300 baskets a week! With money rolling in, Marge and Harry never looked back.

It's one thing to be an experienced Financial Analyst with years of corporate experience and college degrees like Charles and Dalal. But Marge had been a housewife her whole life and never worked outside the home. If Marge can do it, you can do it too! If Susan's grandmother were here, she would tell you what she always told Susan, "Necessity is the mother of invention." And she was right! First Gear needs are what press us to gear up to create a new business or a new life.

If Marge can do it, you can do it too

Harry was in 1st Gear, anxious and afraid. Instead of success, he saw disaster in the making. That imagined future failure kept turning him back. It took time for him to embrace Marge's new positive view. Fortunately Marge's professor and classmates were there for her and for her dream. They were her cheerleaders. They had helped her create it and they could see, hear and feel it in detail.

Co-dreamers, people who hold the details of your dream with you, are essential for creation and innovation. On the journey from an idea to a reality, you will inevitably run into people who will try to dissuade you. People who, in the name of love and caring, will tell you all the "good reason" why you are going to fail! All the reasons why—for their comfort and safety and yours—they think you should turn back! That's when you need to give your Co-dreamer a call so he or she can re-install the details and the enthusiasm you had until you were exposed to that negative view.

Like a skillful driver, Marge was able to shift at the right time. Confronted with financial crisis, she shifted into 3rd Gear to dream a new destination. As the mother of four kids, she'd done that many times over the years. When a broken bone prevented her son from playing in his eagerly-anticipated football game or a fever meant her daughter couldn't go to the prom, Marge had been able to go into their "inner computers" with them and re-imagine and reinforce the details of their dream so they could achieve it another way, another day. She had been able to gear down to lead them through doubts and fears on the first day of school, before exams or their first month away at college. She had supported them in taking each of the steps needed to become productive and competitive. And, year after year, she held their dreams when they couldn't, when fears overtook them or failures made them unable to see success ahead.

In their marriage, Harry led Marge and the kids many times. But now he was the one with rheumatoid arthritis, the one who had been forced to leave his job. So Marge took the lead: She learned the basics in her course; she developed a sound business plan and followed it step by step; she got up and going each and every day. And somewhere along the way, Harry kicked into gear too, shopping and delivering. Despite what their 2nd Gear banker believed, Marge was able to carry over the Success and Leadership Skills she had used at home… into her business.

Thirty-second commercials and 30-minute TV shows give us a false impression about the creation process and the persistent and purposeful step-by-step, day-by-day actions that are required. So, unlike Marge and Harry, most people quit before success arrives! Yes, the idea comes instantaneously, but the process takes time, sometimes lots of it, as the next story will show you.

"A MetLife Inc. survey found that 48% of U.S. workers believe
they will have to take on part-time or full-time work
to maintain their financial stability in retirement."

Wall Street Journal, February 6, 2004

Part Three

The 3rd Gear of Success
and its essential companion—

the 3rd Gear of Leadership

Overview: 3rd Gear Success—
Dreaming and Creating

The shift from 1st to 2nd usually occurs because a leader shifts you... s/he graduates you, certifies you, or lets you know that you've completed a training or educational program. But the shift to 3rd Gear is one you must choose to make yourself...

- when accumulated observations and insights morph into invention and discovery.
- when an idea wakes you in the night or grabs your attention in the hall.
- when you're working along and a better way occurs to you.
- when that new idea leaves you charged, energized and sleepless.
- when you play it in your mind over and over, in more and more detail.
- when you begin reaching out to find Co-dreamers and collaborators.
- when you feel compelled to take action to make your idea a reality.

Can you hold your outcome, mission, goal or dream, not just at the beginning but all the way to completion? Or...

- will obstacles and roadblocks become the reasons your give up?
- will discomfort and disagreement dissuade you or change your mind?
- will it be a 1st or 2nd Gear outcome one rather than a 3rd Gear one?

- will your outcome be the safe and familiar or will it be your dream?
- will it be an outcome someone else has in mind that you don't even want?
- will you trust that, with a clear idea in mind, you will find appropriate methods?
- will you listen to your intuitions and hunches?
- will you let chance and coincidence guide you?
- will you remain committed to your outcome and stay flexible about methods?
- will you stay focused on what and not how?

To operate in 3rd Gear...

- you will need the self-confidence to hold your dream for as long as it takes.
- you will need the personal power to take the necessary steps despite your day to day pressures and workload.
- you will need to believe in your outcome despite the disagreement of people around you...that's not right, that won't work, you don't have the time, skill, money, experience... to do that, what are you thinking?
- If you fail to act, "your idea" will fade from your mind until you hear about someone who responded to their hunch and invented Teflon, Post-It Notes. Or someone who let go of a job he or she didn't want and created one he or she did.

In 3rd Gear, you realize that "everything is connected to everything else..."

- everything you see, hear or feel offers clues to what you're creating.
- everyone you talk to brings new information.
- traffic jams, delays and obstacles become inspirational.
- in 3rd Gear, you realize what a fertile mind you have.
- having birthed a new idea, you must now become a leader—a champion and spokesperson, a nurturer and protector, an implementer and team builder, a production and marketing director, a politician and coach.
- even a conversation you hear in an elevator can trigger your next realization and step.

To complete this idea, you will need to find Co-dreamers...

- people who are willing, and able, to hold your dream with you.
- people who will meet with you to give your idea additional detail and power.
- people you can call after a bad break and your idea feels like it's been erased from your mind.
- people who will "reinstall" the details you have Co-dreamed with them.
- people who will revitalize your dream and give it power.
- people who will help you network to find the support, expertise and money you will need to move from start to realization and enjoyment.
- people who can operate in 3rd Gear in their own lives and businesses.
- people who have a vision of a successful future.
- people who believe in the inherent creativity of all people.
- people who can see the Big Picture.
- people who understand that innovation is the key to our future.
- The 3rd Gear of Success is alive and inspiring...
- in it you will discover your passion and mission.
- your new idea may offer you the opportunity you've been longing for... the opportunity to change your life, your business and world.
- will you seize this opportunity... or will you let it pass?
- everyone shifts into 3rd Gear from time to time, everyone can create new ideas.
- but not everyone takes the actions needed to bring the idea into reality.
- the path to your dream is not a well-marked highway.
- it weaves and meanders and even goes backwards at times.
- your dream will wake you up in the night.
- even if you swear off of it, it will come back. Your dream has a life of its own.
- the only way to proceed now is to focus on your dream and let it guide you there.

3rd Gear Word Signals: The following words let you know when you or someone else is operating in 3rd Gear...

Aha!, insight, realize, imagine, dream, create plan, intend, communicate, collaborate, detail, team building, interested, open, listening, flexible, responsive, respect, trust, include, cooperate, innovate, co-dream, co-create, chance, serendipity, synchronicity, coincidence, intuit, putting 2 and 2 together, whole, holographic, out of the blue, magic, inner guidance, inner knower, co-creating with a Higher Power, too far out there, in a dream world, a space head, a hopeless dreamer, full of hair brained schemes, can't pay the bills, a constant loser, out of it.

These words give you a feel for what is most desirable — and most destructive — about 3rd Gear, depending on how sensitively you use it.

Remember: If you don't know what you want... in detail... then you'll probably get what someone else wants. Possibly someone who wants you to shift back into 1st or 2nd Gear with him or her. Or someone who wants you to complete his/her dream instead of yours.

The more you can see, hear, feel and prelive what you have in mind, the greater the probability that you will experience those results — positive or negative. Therefore, dream and don't dread. Let your detailed ideas guide you to the realities you want at work, at home, in your community and world.

"Imagination will often carry us to worlds that never were.
But without it, we go nowhere."

Carl Sagan
American astronomer, astrophysicist, cosmologist, author, science popularizer and communicator

Unemployed and Starting Over

A t 55, Jenny Masters was a sophisticated lady with a radiant smile. She was able to quote Shakespeare in one breath and tell you where the Bach Society was having its Friday concert in the next. Jenny was a successful immigration attorney. For the last twenty-two years, she and her husband Rodney had built a highly profitable practice. Together they had developed a set of business strategies that worked and the money had rolled in. Then Rodney found a new love in his life and their marriage ended. Jenny understood it was over and, with no regrets, she moved on.

In their settlement, she gave Rodney her half of the practice in exchange for the liquid assets she would need to start again. For the next several months, Jenny attended lunches and dinners with lawyers and headhunters waiting for the next career opportunity to pop up. But nothing did. Her legal friends ended each meal with, "Let me know where you land" but they never offered to hire her. Head-hunters told her that at 55 she was too old to find a job in Corporate America… unless she underwent plastic surgery so they could pass her off as younger. When she said she was unwilling, they concluded her best bet was to start her own practice. But that wasn't appealing.

After several months, Jenny realized she was stuck and a friend advised her to hire a life coach to help her make this transition more easily. After a week of screening and interviewing four or five candidates, she chose Brit Carlson who lived on the West coast, but since their conversations would be by phone, the distance didn't matter.

During the first call, Brit took careful notes on her background and strengths and then asked Jenny to take some time to visualize her perfect job, the one she dreamed of having at this time in her life. Jenny spent one week thinking and pre-experiencing. She decided she could clearly see herself working in the marketing department of an international company, traveling the world, doing deals and being handsomely paid. "Why does that dream feel right?" Brit wanted to know. "Because I'm a great negotiator and, with my legal expertise, I know how to structure deals. And I love doing them," Jenny came back strongly.

"Wonderful. So now that you have a dream, what's the first tiny step you can take in that direction?" Brit asked. "But, but… Brit, wait a minute, you don't understand. You have to know people to get that kind of job. I don't know anyone who has connections like that," Jenny responded fearfully.

"Jenny, here's the bottom line. You're not too old to start a practice and enjoy building it. You're not too old to work for an international company and travel the world. But you may be too scared. When we are scared, it's easier to find reasons why not, than to imagine steps we can take. "Does that ring true for you?" he asked. "Yes, it sure does. I'm scared to death, scared to take action even in the direction of a dream. That's why I hired you. I need your help," she confided.

"Before you decide to move in that direction, Jenny; before you decide to confront your fears and move up, over, around or through them, take a deep look inside and answer this question, 'Do you really want the dream position you described?" asked Brit. "Yes. I really do. I'm single. I'm smart and I want to travel and enjoy exciting days ahead," Jenny reaffirmed. "Okay, then let's get started," Brit announced. "Here's your first step. Go to your local library or do a search on your computer. Find seven international marketing companies for which you would like to work. Get as many details as you can on each one and the type of international trade in which they're engaged. Call me when you've completed that step... when you're successful."

Four days later, Jenny called back. "Did you get the full name, address, phone numbers, financial and other details about these companies?" Brit asked immediately. "Yes", Jenny responded. "Well done," he said with a smile. They discussed the limiting emotions she'd had to move through to take each of those steps. Brit praised her and labeled each step she had taken "a success" — a successful step in the direction she wanted to go. Then he asked if she was ready for her next assignment. Now that she was feeling successful and confident, she was ready to move ahead. "OK, now call each company and get the name of the VP of Marketing."

Brit guided Jenny and acknowledged her progress step-by-step and call-by-call. His instructions were quite specific like "Go back to your library or to your computer and scan through all the business journals that pertain to the markets in which these seven companies trade. When you find something interesting, make a copy or print it on your printer. Once a week, send one or two of the most relevant and interesting articles to each of these VPs along with your business card and a note simply stating, 'Thought this might interest you.'" He instructed her to repeat this once a week for seven weeks. "Then on week eight, call each VP and make an appointment to talk."

Of the seven VPs that Jenny phoned, three agreed to see her... mainly out of curiosity. Next, Brit taught her how to handle the upcoming interviews: how to talk straight, how to explain the position she was searching for, how to spell out why she was qualified and what benefits she would bring to their company. Jenny and Brit spent hours on the phone together roleplaying successful interviews before she finally went to meet the three VP's.

Jenny was surprised to discover that, from the three interviews, she received two offers. The first position paid next to nothing, but the second one fit her dream nicely and she accepted it. After the interview, Chuck

Dickerson, the VP of Marketing, let Jenny know that no one on his staff of fifteen had sent him any interesting articles in the last 12 months… and they were being well-paid to keep him informed. He said he was so impressed with her initiative that he just had to meet her. He felt that with her background and qualifications, she would be quite successful in the position. "I'm starting work in two weeks," she shared enthusiastically.

Jenny couldn't thank Brit enough. Yes, she'd had doubts about hiring a coach at first but she had faithfully followed his advice and it paid off handsomely! She was back in action!

Moving past fears to futures

Together Jenny and her husband had run a successful practice for 22 years, but she didn't want to run that practice alone and she wasn't sure she had the motivation and staying power to start over someplace else. Her fears were reinforced by her lawyer and headhunter friends who told her she was too old for Corporate America and urged Jenny to have cosmetic surgery to look younger. But that was not an idea she could buy.

After months of fruitless efforts, Jenny decided to follow a friend's advice and hire a life coach who was skilled in guiding individuals and teams from ideas to implementation. As a skillful 1st Gear Leader, Brit knew he would need to guide Jenny ahead… successful-step by-successful step… and build her self-confidence at the same time. Without self-confidence, she could have all the skills and talents in the world but not be able to complete the actions that would be needed to turn them into a job… and income.

Once you have a dream, old fears, doubts, failures, limits and patterns come up to haunt you. To move ahead, you need to learn how to update your old "programming" or find an expert who can update it with you. An expert you can put your confidence in until you build confidence in yourself and your intuitions in this new area.

"Unless you are prepared to give up something valuable
you will never be able to truly change at all, because you'll be forever in the
control of things you can't give up."

Andy Law, author of *Creative Company*

Franchised but Scared to Gear Down

Pete peered out his office window on downtown Chicago. It was winter again and he could see warmly wrapped people rushing in the streets below. Then his eyes darted back to his computer and the advertising copy he was working on. After thirteen years as chief copywriter for Newbolt, Macy & Owen, a small ad agency, he felt he was churning out more of the same year after year, though he had to admit that he still had a flair for making it look good and sound fresh.

"It's time for a change," he thought, as he headed for the coffee machine. "What does success mean to me at this point in my life? What do I really want?" Back at his desk, he wrote: "Be my own boss and make some serious money." Later that night in their apartment off Lake Shore Drive, Pete told his wife Sally he'd gone as far as he could and was making as much money as the agency would ever pay him. "But Pete, it's a good job. What more do you want?" Sally asked. "Well, I need to work on my own and prove to myself that I can start a successful business," he answered. Sally was an accountant and she knew the statistics for startups only too well. "Do you realize there's a 60%-80% failure rate for new businesses each year in this country?" "Sure, but what makes you think that will apply to us?" "Starting a new business is something you need to think through. You don't even know what type of business you'd like to start, Pete. Don't expect me to give up my day job!" The matter ended there… for the night.

A few days later, Pete was glancing through Income Opportunities Magazine. It contained a section that said franchising startups had an 80% success rate. With a franchise, you're buying the right to operate a business designed by someone who has tackled and solved the problems most people encounter. With a franchise, you're purchasing a head start to success and an expert support system. Here was the answer for which Pete had been looking. He showed Sally the article and she agreed that franchising was a much safer bet. But was he going to buy another Wendy's or McDonalds? No, Pete had heard about a franchising expo at the Convention Center, and he talked Sally into going with him.

They were amazed at the variety of businesses that were available, well over 300. Pete was drawn to a travel franchise called Cruise Away. The figures for the cruise industry were compelling. Studies show that taking a cruise is the dream of 50% of all adults, especially Baby Boomers. With only 12.5% of the U.S. population having ever taken a cruise, it seemed the market was untapped. By year-end 2004, it was projected that 9 million passengers would be cruising each year. He spoke to their sales representative and took home brochures to study. Pete felt he could do well with this. "It's a $35,000 investment and I can start working from home. With my writing skills, I'll have it making money in no time," he told Sally. "But honey, they don't want you to be creative. They want you to follow their rules. This is a franchise and you're buying their system and expertise. You will have to do it their way for it to sail," she reminded him knowing how much Pete loved reinventing the wheel.

Perhaps warm tropical Bahamian air has an extra appeal when you're bundled up in a Chicago winter. Whether that was it or not, within a month Pete had resigned and was in Cruise Away's ten-day training program at their corporate office in Detroit. There was a lot to learn and absorb every day. And he spent hours at night in his hotel room familiarizing himself with his new industry so he would be up and running by the time he got home.

Four weeks later, he had stationery printed, his computer was installed, and he was ready to make sales. But people don't walk off the street to book cruises; he would have to reach out to them. He knew how to write copy so he wrote three small ads and placed them in the local paper. After four weeks with next to no results, he rewrote the copy, but his phone still wasn't ringing.

"Pete, you need to call Cruise Away. It's been three months now and you haven't made a cent," she stated flatly, "And I'm concerned about our financial future." The next day, Pete spoke with the business development manager for his region. He would be in Chicago in five days so they scheduled an appointment to talk. Fred Stroller was a no-nonsense sort of guy. After a few pleasantries, they got down to work.

Opening Pete's file and starting down a long checklist, Fred asked to see his ads. Pete proudly showed him the three he had written and run. "No, not these ads. I want to see the ads with the copy we sent you," Fred stated flatly. Pete told him he knew the advertising business and his own ads were superior.

Fred quickly explained that Pete had just broken the first rule of franchising—believing that you know a better way. "You see, Pete, what you actually bought is our way, a way we've spent millions of dollars developing, testing and refining. That's why Cruise Away franchises work. As soon as you change the formula, you're asking for trouble."

Sally didn't have to say I told you so but she did. "You changed their copy and no one responded. That's what they taught me in business school: First, follow the rules. And in this case, their rules cost us $35,000! Besides since half the money is mine, don't you think you should take me on a cruise to familiarize us with the product?"

Two weeks later, they sailed out of Port Everglades, Florida for St. Maarten. The weather was glorious, the food never-ending, the entertainment top-notch. The first day at sea, Sally and Pete attended our workshop *The Three Gears of Success* and over lunch they discussed what we had covered.

"So Pete, now do you see that franchises are for people who can operate in 1st Gear, people who can learn the rules and use them to become productive," chided Sally. "You've had a 3rd Gear job since I met you. But to succeed in this new venture, you will have to gear down before you can gear up." Pete nodded sheepishly as he sipped a daiquiri, munched on banana fritters and scanned the horizon.

Feeling a little seasick and far sicker at heart, Pete realized he wouldn't be able to start his business in 3rd Gear. He thought for a minute or two about giving Newbolt, Macy & Owen a call to see if his old job was still open. But he decided to stay the course, knowing there'd be a time and place for his 3rd Gear skills... later on. He realized his discomfort with 1st and 2nd Gears had been limiting him until now, preventing him from learning new things and increasing his position and income.

He refocused on his dream: I want to prove to myself that I can build a successful business and make some serious money. But now he knew that completing it would require not just the gear he most enjoyed, but all three gears used at the right time. With $35,000 riding on it, he chose to gear down and start over. And Sally was impressed.

1st Gear comes first... whether you like It or not

Things changed dramatically in Sally and Pete's thinking as soon as they heard our talk. Finally Sally had the information she needed to help Pete understand why she had told him to follow the franchise's directions exactly. She wasn't being negative; she was being business-smart. After years with Pete, she knew only too well that he was uncomfortable in 1st and 2nd Gears so he had chosen creative jobs that allowed him to operate in 3rd Gear most of the time. But their future depended on his ability to shift down into 1st Gear. Their $35,000 investment would go up in smoke if he couldn't get his franchise started properly.

Fortunately Fred, the Cruise Away manager, quickly brought Pete back to the reality of what it takes to start a franchise. Fred obviously faces this challenge with franchisees on an on-going basis. Having a name for the 1st Gear of Success, as well as the 2nd and 3rd, will make it far easier for him to explain why he is so focused on rules and regulations during start-up.

Advertising people, like Pete, frequently fail to understand the problems business people face day to day. How many times have you seen glamorous models on TV promising exceptional service only to face the reality of a nightmarish shopping experience—a product that wasn't delivered on time and didn't live up to advertised expectations?

Which gears do we need to be responsible for when we advertise—1st, 2nd or 3rd? The truth is, we must be responsible for all three. The product or service must be safe and effective; the price must be fair and competitive;

and the product must meet the dream we planted in our customers' mind through our ad or sales presentation.

It is essential to understand the Three Gears of Success and Leadership not just at work but also at home. What are the expectations we must live up to with our families? What promises—spoken and unspoken—must we be able to keep?

"The franchise entrepreneurial spirit in the United States has never been more alive than today. Forty-five hundred franchise businesses with 600,000 outlets crowd the marketplace, accounting for a third of all retail sales nationwide."

Franchising: Pathway to Wealth Creation
Spinelli et al, 2004

Overview: 3rd Gear Leadership—Co-Dreaming and Co-Creating

When is 3rd Gear Leadership needed?

- when someone you are leading has a new idea that hits him or her in the night, in the shower, at work, or in the car.
- when someone is presenting a new idea or concept and you need to remain open.
- when s/he needs you to experience what it looks, sounds and feels like in detail, and precisely what it will do and contribute to your organization or community.
- when s/he needs you to set aside time to understand its implications, to imagine its impact and contribution.
- when s/he needs you to make time to Co-dream and Co-create in detail.
- when s/he needs you to add details and additional perspective and experience.
- when s/he needs you to understand that if this idea isn't it, the next one may be.
- when someone needs you to realize that nothing happens without a dream.
- when someone needs you to remember when you had a valuable dream
- when s/he needs you to remember that what was impossible yesterday may be possible now.

What do you need to be aware of in the 3rd Gear of Leadership?

- many brilliant ideas for methods, products and systems go un-nurtured.
- or, worse, they are brutally stomped out at the start.
- to succeed in business and to keep up and move ahead as a nation, we will need to be able to shift up into 3rd Gear Leadership to continue innovating and leading.
- the timing of the shift to 3rd Gear is subtle.
- it can't be predicted or planned.
- it seems to happen at the "wrong time" but the timing is always perfect... in retrospect.

What does someone in 3rd Gear need from you?

- give them the time and freedom to develop their ideas.
- allow them to collaborate with others in your organization who have expertise.
- dream their dream with them.
- see their "future reality" in your mind in as much detail as possible, prelive it with them.
- ask questions to clarify what it looks, sounds and feels like, what it will do specifically.
- hold the details of their dream for them when they get discouraged or overwhelmed, when they are tempted to give up.
- remind them of the power of their dream.
- point out the successes they are having along the way.
- suggest that they read stories about great inventors and inventions to inspire them.
- give them examples of dreamers who have changed your organization, whether they were "the lowest man on the totem pole" or someone in the R&D.
- go to the store and see how many new products are on the shelves.
- make a list of everything you have created in your life... no matter when.
- remind them that someday people will be unable to remember what life was like without this idea, method or product, without this way of thinking, living and being.
- let them know that there's nothing more fulfilling than bringing a dream into reality.

- remember: Invention is "1% inspiration and 99% perspiration" according to Thomas Edison if you can dream it, you can do it… if you are committed and you can use all three gears.

3rd Gear Word Signals: The following words let you know when you or someone else is operating in 3rd Gear…

Aha!, insight, realize, imagine, dream, create plan, intend, communicate, collaborate, detail, team building, interested, open, listening, flexible, responsive, respect, trust, include, cooperate, innovate, co-dream, co-create, chance, serendipity, synchronicity, coincidence, intuit, putting 2 and 2 together, whole, holographic, out of the blue, magic, inner guidance, inner knower, co-creating with a Higher Power, too far out there, in a dream world, a space head, a hopeless dreamer, full of hair brained schemes, can't pay the bills, a constant loser, out of it

These words give you a feel for what is most desirable — and most destructive — about 3rd Gear, depending on how sensitively you use it.

As a 3rd Gear leader, ask yourself and others…

- what problems are you facing in your company or family?
- what problems are you confronting in your community, country and world?
- what are you able to contribute? What expertise do you bring?
- what are we telling ourselves is impossible?
- what do we need to change to live more fulfilling lives?
- what resources, informational and material, do we need and where are they?
- what trends are emerging?
- what diseases are affecting us?
- what are we eating, drinking and breathing, and how is it impacting us?
- what is happening to our weather and environment?
- how will the demographics affect you and your organization?
- what is occurring in the global marketplace that will impact your   supplies, workforce and economy?
- what media messages are influencing your culture and marketplace?
- what complaints do you regularly receive?
- what are your products unable to do?
- what is missing in your facility or plant?

- what are your vendors and customers asking you for?
- what services are your competitors offering that you are not?
- who is creating new methods and systems that could be useful to you?
- what will you need to do that you are not preparing for now?
- what education and training do you and your team need to compete and lead?
- who has an insight, understanding, idea or plan that needs your support now?

"Now more than ever, innovation is the answer. Jobs will arise from the creation of new products, processes, and markets."

Robert D. Hof, *Business Week*, March 1, 2004

Viva the Red Firecracker

Hotel Corporation of America owned and managed 156 properties across the U.S. The majority of the hotels were profitable, but a half dozen dragged down the company's bottom line. Buffalo had one such problem hotel and it was decided that something had to be done and fast. So Betty Lou Day, the "red firecracker" manager, flew there to turn things around.

Five foot two and 190 pounds with flaming red hair, this dynamo moved at a rapid clip, talked at breakneck speed and never forgot a name. She had joined Hotel Corporation as a trainee at 18 and at 46 she was without doubt their 'top gun.'

As soon as the Red Firecracker pulled up at the Downtown Inn in central Buffalo, she called a meeting of the department heads: Food and Beverages, Sales, Front Desk, Housekeeping Maintenance and Security. The speculation was feverish. They knew her reputation and hoped she could save their hotel and their jobs. And after a warm welcome, she got right down to work. "First I want each of you to meet with your teams and go over their job descriptions. Make sure they know what their job is and precisely how you want them to do it. And if you need to retrain them, get started. Make sure you communicate with them at least twice a day and let them know when they've done a good job." Betty Lou had coffee and Danish with the department heads later that day and got their candid feedback on what they thought was working and not working at the hotel. Within two weeks the staff had received updated copies of their job descriptions and, where necessary, they had been retrained to accomplish them. The daily communication with staff was already improving morale.

The hotel executive team met once a week. At those meetings Betty Lou began painting a vision of a prosperous hotel full of exciting activities, 100% room occupancy, happy returning guests and a great place to work. She brought them all into her dream by spelling it out in detail so they could each see, hear, smell, taste and touch it. Bottom line, so they could pre-experience it. Then, to make sure they were all in alignment, she had each member playback the vision to the group and they added even more details as they were doing this. It was a magical and transformative journey they were on. None of them had ever experienced a leader like this; they adored her and daily went the extra mile to bring their shared vision into reality.

Betty Lou then joined the Buffalo Chamber of Commerce so she could meet the local movers and shakers. After attending two meetings, she selected four key players: Dave Jackson, who owned the local golf club; Millie Andrews, president of a large pet food manufacturer; Carlos Munda who ran a small bus company, and Leslie Green, who was the head of the local tourist bureau. Betty Lou invited them all to lunch at the hotel. She had Chef Carpenter prepare an impressive meal and, delighted with the challenge, he enthusiastically and creatively exceeded her expectations. After enjoying drinks and a fabulous lunch, Betty Lou began, "We all have something in common: We want to revitalize Buffalo. Am I right?" Five heads nodded in agreement. "Well, here's what I suggest. Let's create a major annual event like a golf tournament. Dave has a first-class golf course to hold it on. Millie can take some money from her advertising budget and offer a $5,000 first prize and a 'Chow, Chow Foods Trophy.' Our hotel will have all our rooms available at huge discount prices. Carlos will provide the transportation from the airport to the hotel and the hotel to the golf course. Leslie will get the promotion ball rolling across the state... and we're in business." Betty Lou looked around the room and saw five pairs of eyes light up. She had her Co-dreamers and they immediately started working on the details.

Back at the hotel, Betty Lou started with Sales. "Let's take the top floor and reserve it for business guests only. We will have newspapers and magazines as well as fresh fruit, coffee and cake available all day. Each room will need to have high-speed internet service." Soon Maintenance, Food and Beverage, and Sales were working on a shared vision for the new luxury executive suites. Next, she asked her Sales Team to scan the local papers for engagement announcements and to send each couple an engraved invitation to a complimentary lunch and champagne. Once they were enjoying themselves at the hotel, the Sales Department offered wedding specials which included the reception hall and band, special rates for guest rooms, and a free wedding cake. Who could resist? And soon Sales was booking five weddings a month.

Betty Lou poured through the yellow pages looking for a building supply company that could deliver five truckloads of sand. After negotiating the best price, she arranged to have the sand dumped next to the outdoor bar. With her "beach" on its way, she called a talent agency and booked "The Four Jamaican Men" and started advertising her Friday "Buffalo to Bahamas Night" in the local paper. The bartender made up Bahamian cocktails and she had a volleyball net installed in the sand so customers could take their shoes off and play. She sponsored a "Best Dressed Caribbean" competition with dinner for four in the hotel restaurant as a prize. Drinks were two for one from 5:00 to 6:00 pm. The band played, the liquor flowed, and the customers came and stayed. It was the 'in place" to be on Friday nights and liquor sales went through the roof. Yes, the Red Firecracker had arrived and she was exploding.

Chef Carpenter was the next person on Betty Lou's list. Together they worked out a three-course business lunch served from noon to 2:00 daily. They low-balled it at $6.00 and made it up on beverage sales. It was a runaway success with the local business people. Then, buoyed up by that success, she and Chef Carpenter created theme nights for the restaurant. Monday was French, Tuesday was Italian, Wednesday was Chinese and so it went, filling all those once empty chairs and making everyone on the team confident and proud to be on the Downtown Inn Buffalo team.

She geared up and they geared up with her

Betty Lou Day was able to use all three gears and shift them when appropriate. From the start, she made her management team feel important; she shared and listened, directed and corrected, and took time to provide positive feedback to build their confidence and enthusiasm. Within weeks she had helped them rebuild their foundation, replacing shaky 1st Gear job descriptions and unclear communications with a thoroughly talked-through vision of an attractive successful future.

The Red Firecracker utilized her resources inside and outside the hotel. Once she had her people back on track and her systems in place, she began generating 3rd Gear ideas — ideas to boost sales and bring in new business. And she Co-dreamed with her team not just to get them on board, but so they could begin generating approaches of their own. The synergy was contagious and so was the success!

Not only did Betty Lou give her staff the kind of Three-Gear Leadership they needed, but she also put herself in her customers' shoes and provided the services and experiences they wanted. They were happy to spend, spend, spend at the annual golf weekend, daily business lunches, and international dinners. Having experienced a tantalizing sample, they brought Betty Lou their wedding and celebration events too, and they kept coming back when she delivered as promised. When they were thinking ahead to fun times with friends and family they chose to spend those specials moments at the Downtown Inn. Betty Lou was able to help the community and its leaders see what the Downtown Inn could contribute to Buffalo.

The Red Firecracker turned a loss into a profit. But she didn't just lead her team into 2nd Gear and endlessly push them longer and harder. She "visioned" them into 3rd Gear, suggesting smart solutions and inviting them to Co-dream and Co-create those realities. And, each step of the way, no matter which Success Gear they were in, Betty Lou let them know they were successful.

"The best and most sustainable innovation occurs
where creativity and customer needs intersect."

**W. James McNerney, Jr., Chairman and CEO
3M Company**

Esprit Miami: A New Idea Blooms

Around Miami International Airport, there are two hundred or so flower wholesalers. Each day they fly in fresh-cut flowers from Columbia and Ecuador. Once the flowers clear customs, they are trucked into industrial coolers to be stored until their sales teams can distribute them to wholesalers around the country. Cut-flowers are perishable so, as the day fades, importers adjust prices to clear their inventory. Prices go down steadily unless other factors intervene.

After working for a leading wholesaler to learn the business, in 1980 Christine Martindale decided to start her own company, Esprit Miami. Christine had very limited startup capital and business training, but with vision and determination she entered this highly competitive field and started developing a sales force. They were all up before dawn, hitting the phones and building their client base. Christine had early setbacks: "I was honest and I expected my customers would pay. I had a lot of people who didn't pay the first year. In that year, I lost four times my entire investment," Christine recalls. So she reached out to experts and engaged the services of a credit agency that kept tabs on her client's credit histories. Then she could refocus on sales.

In 1985, Richard began working with Christine to enhance the skills of her sales team. By then, her sales were exceeding $7 million and she had over 300 active accounts. Christine had learned to sense when she needed to shift into 1st Gear to patiently explain how each job had to be done and when to shift to 2nd to motivate her team to clear the day's inventory.

With 200 plus importers, the competition was brutal. Christine realized it would be important for her to find ways to distinguish Esprit Miami from the rest of the pack. One day she woke up thinking about 'designer flowers.' They would be the perfect accessory to fashion clothing in stores. This would be her competitive edge.

Christine quickly shifted into 3rd Gear and sought advice from a fashion forecast company. Fashion colors had to be decided well in advance so factories would have sufficient time to manufacture the clothing. With these understandings in hand, she flew to visit her South American suppliers. It was a gamble for those farms to grow 'designer colors' but Christine was persuasive and promised to purchase their full production.

Next season Esprit Miami was the only wholesaler offering 'designer flowers.' With no competition, Christine set her prices and put her company on the map. The other 200 importers were stuck in 2nd Gear fighting it out on price. But Christine was able to shift into 3rd Gear with stunning success. It shows that creative thinking is the ultimate marketing tool. Looking back,

Christine said, "I realized that I was in a competitive business. If I could get some small advantage just to give me an edge, then I would have a chance."

She let her dream guide her

Christine's leadership skills speak for themselves. She was a Three-Gear Leader capable of shifting into whichever gear was needed at the time. Once she had her 1st Gear foundation in place, instead of pushing longer and harder in a highly competitive marketplace and burning her people out, she implemented a new idea—one that was solidly grounded in 2nd Gear understandings. She knew her South American growers wouldn't be interested in planting experimental "designer flowers" unless she committed to purchasing the whole crop. The guaranteed sale made it safe for them to engage in her dream. No, Christine didn't know how to pull this off... all by herself. She reached out to experts to provide the specialized information she needed on advanced selling skills, fashion colors for the upcoming season, and how to accurately assess her customers' ability to pay.

One of the primary skills of creative leaders is their ability to generate such a detailed, well-formed dream that they can "live" in that dream until they can bring it into reality, and they can bring others into that dream with them. Instead of focusing their attention on fears or what might go wrong, they commit to their dream. They give people around them the opportunity to make this magical leap of faith with them. No, the realization of a dream doesn't just happen... poof! It takes systems and information, powerful Co-dreamers, consistent focused hard work and the ability, moment by moment, to shift up and down into whichever gear is needed.

Most people don't realize that there are Three Success and Leadership Gears, so they habitually use the one or two that are familiar to them. Like drivers who don't have all the gears working in their transmission, they are unable to move ahead smoothly and efficiently. And they do the same things the same way... day after day... even though they aren't getting the results they want.

We are in the midst of a paradigm shift. Our old logic and systems are not able to keep up with the changes we're confronting—not just in our towns and cities but all over the world. Because of the internet, overnight deliveries, modems, computers and interconnected systems, an idea created anywhere in the world can be an idea you can quickly use and profit from if you are willing. But will you stay open to new ideas? But will you stay open to finding the expertise you need? And will you have the courage to reach out and grasp it... wherever it is? The courage to keep learning and changing?

Despite all the changes, certain foundational values never change: integrity, cooperation, full communication and trust. Without a solid 1st Gear foundation in place, our more-better-fast-cheaper structure is subject to collapse and disaster. But with that foundation in place, we can work together to solve any problem that confronts us. Above all, we are creators and to move beyond our current limits, we must regularly engage... and trust... our creativity and the creativity of everyone around us.

"Capital isn't so important in business. Experience isn't so important. You can get both these things. What is important is ideas. If you have ideas, you have the main asset you need, and there isn't any limit to what you can do with your business and your life."

Harvey Firestone, founder
Firestone Tire and Rubber Company

Cleaner than Clean

At 32, Steve was smarting from his second divorce. The first was painful, but this one was far worse. Steve was in a custody battle for his five-year-old son Jimmy and his life had cracked wide open.

Steve finished high school and went to work in the family mortgage business. With interest rates low, everyone wanted to refinance. But dressing up in a suit and tie, heading into the office, and being strapped to a desk wasn't Steve's cup to tea. So as he answered the same old mortgage questions, he spent hours each day dreaming his perfect job.

Then it happened. He headed over to Valley Park to get some papers signed and decided to stop at Wendy's for lunch. Sitting by the window munching a taco salad and sipping a diet soda, he was staring blankly across the street when suddenly his eyes focused. There in the National Bank parking lot was a truck just like his except it had a high-pressure cleaning unit attached to the back. A guy in jeans and a white vest was cleaning the walls of the bank. "Wow!" he mumbled as his mind began racing. "That guy spends his days driving around in his truck, working outdoors, and he's in business for himself. That would be a fun way for me to make a living!"

Steve couldn't sleep that night. He kept tossing and turning. Finally he surrendered and turned on the light and wrote a list of information he would need to start his own cleaning business: how much the equipment would cost, the licenses and insurance required. He wondered how much business owners pay to have their buildings cleaned. Then a sizzling idea popped into mind. "I've helped mortgage lots of buildings over the years. They all need to be cleaned and I know the owners. Holy cow, I've got a ready-made client base." Jumping on the internet, he discovered that two thousand dollars worth of equipment would have him up and running. Then, to test the viability of his idea, he called three former clients. They told him they would be happy to give him their business... if his price was right.

With his divorce complete, it was time to make changes. He was single again and sure he would soon have custody of his son. He had the energy and capital needed to start his own business.

His family was shocked but not surprised. They knew Steve's heart had never been in selling mortgages. Accepting his decision, his father said, "I want to give you some advice. You know little or nothing about this new venture, son. Study it in detail before you spend your money."

Steve converted his den to an office and bought a computer and a three-in-one printer/fax/scanner. He incorporated Steve's Cleaning Service and made "Cleaner than Clean" his slogan. He purchased accounting software, obtained his Federal Tax ID number and opened a business account with his slogan printed on his checks.

Soon Steve was obsessed with valves, plungers, wands, pumps, nozzles, guns and hoses. When he was sure what he needed, he bought a 5.5 HP Honda cleaning unit and had it fitted to his truck. But he soon realized equipment costs were only a small portion of his overall expenses. In his family's business, his healthcare had been covered. Now he had to fork out $700 a month for his son and him. And he had to buy insurance to cover damage he might do to a building as to himself and others. Then there was the looming custody battle. At a meeting with his attorneys, Moongrove and Sylvester, Steve discovered legal costs would be $30,000 he didn't have. He would need to take a personal loan. But, despite all this, he was determined to make Cleaner than Clean a success.

Finally ready, Steve's first cleaning job was a three-story building in Park Town West. What a learning experience that was! Steve underestimated how long it would take and so he under priced the whole job. Fun, no not exactly. At the end of three days of holding the high pressure hose, his back ached but he was happy. He was doing what he wanted to do and doing it on his own. Cleaning buildings all day was tough but coming home to handle the phone calls, paperwork, billing and marketing that came along with running a business was much tougher!

Moongrove and Sylvester finally came through and Jimmy moved in. Parenting brought great pleasure and additional demands. Week days Steve had to take Jimmy to daycare at 8:00 and picked him up at 5:00. This meant he couldn't begin work before 8:30 and had to end by 4:30. He had no flexibility about starting earlier or leaving later. Coming back to finish the job another day added to his expenses.

After three months, an exhausted Steve realized he was in business, but he wasn't making money. Yes, he had lots of clients — more than he could handle — but his expenses were high. If he could only work two more hours a day and Saturdays, he could make a profit. He thought back to that lunch at Wendy's when he saw the vision of his own cleaning business. How fresh and exciting it had been. But a new reality had set in. He would have to work more-better-faster-cheaper if he wanted to survive and thrive in the cleaning business.

The following week, Jimmy was home from daycare with strep throat, and Steve was forced to cancel his jobs and stay with him. The timing was especially frustrating because Steve had just sent out a mailing to his clients that included cleaning private homes as well as commercial properties. Within hours after the mailman delivered his copy of the mailer, the phone started ringing. The first three calls were from homeowners in Fairview, a high-end gated community, Fairview. On the third call he asked a few more questions and discovered that Fairview had over two thousand units and the board of directors had recently mandated that, to maintain the prestigious appearance, homeowners needed to clean their roofs every three years. And Steve realized that dozens of housing developments must have these same rules. "What if I build a relationship with these communities?" he asked himself.

With Jimmy still sick, Steve had time to explore this huge, untapped market. Yes, commercial buildings paid more per job so most contractors focused on them, but what if he specialized on home roofs and did the job better, cheaper and cleaner?

Learning from his past experience, Steve arranged to do the three cleaning jobs at Fairview and made sure all three roofs lived up to his slogan, cleaner than clean, when he finished. Next he analyzed those jobs to determine how much time each roof had taken, what materials he'd used and added on a fair profit. When he was sure what his pricing needed to be, Steve made an appointment with Fairview's Board of Directors, took them to see all three roofs, presented his pricing, and asked to be their "official roof cleaner." His idea worked for everyone, for the community, the homeowner and Steve. Soon he had a steady stream of roofs to clean, not just at Fairview, but at other communities he approached.

Over the months, Steve had gotten to know several other building cleaners. He called each of them and, to his surprise, they were delighted to clean for him on days they had available. Now he was booking work and contracting it out. Sure he could still continue clean buildings himself but he had also created a new division.

The following month, Steve hired Brenda to be his assistant. She called to schedule jobs and assigned them to one of Steve's sub-contractors, all of whom were highly reliable. Brenda was also available to take Jimmy to daycare or pick him up whenever Steve needed more time on a job.

Jimmy's strep throat had been a career-changing opportunity. Staying home with his son that week had given Steve time away from the pressure of cleaning buildings to imagine and implement a new and more profitable way to do business. And Steve's father knew his son had made the right decision. He could see that Steve was happy doing his own business his own way.

Chance events can move us ahead... if we let them

A job—even if it's in your family's business—is not a life sentence. People used to work for the same company their whole lives, but today most people work for many companies during their careers.

When you know something isn't right for you, can you stand up to family and friends, to coworkers and bosses and say, "I don't want to do this anymore"? Or will you, instead, lose your energy and enthusiasm in a determined effort to do what you think you should, what's making you a good living despite your own feelings and health?

The 2003 Spherion Workforce Study shows us that the majority of people in the workplace, The Emerging Workforce, are willing to let go and move ahead. They have the confidence it takes to trust they will find a job that suits them better than the one they don't want, or want but can't have. According to the study, "39% of the workforce has now worked for six or more employers" and "51% of U.S. workers are extremely/very likely to look for a new job or work situation."

Let's look at this in terms of gears. As kids we were expected to do what our parents, teachers and bosses said we should do. To succeed in 1st Gear, that's what we did. But the meaning of success shifts. Being loyal to people's rules was the 1st phase of what we had to do to get ahead but to continue succeeding, we had to shift into 2nd Gear productivity and competitiveness. We had to put in long hours and endure the pressures of deadlines and quotas to get our boss's acknowledgment that we were doing enough, well enough to climb to the next rung of the corporate ladder. If success is only 2nd Gear, we're at risk—at risk of slipping behind on new technologies, at risk of burning ourselves out in the name of perks and prizes, at risk of missing creative opportunities. And, despite our sacrifice to the corporate cause, at risk of being laid off when our job is outmoded or shipped overseas. Today it is no longer enough to be one- or two-gear employees. We must shift the definition of success to the next level and become three-gear employees, individuals who can operate in All Three Success Gears as needed.

Even that's not enough. We must also be able to step up into leadership… not just 1st Gear Leadership where we teach new learners and those who are willing to remain obedient. Not just 2nd Gear Leadership where we manage others to produce results. But into Three-Gear Leadership where we lead first ourselves and then others in all three gears, when we're starting, competing, and when we have a new slant on an old problem that will revolutionize our industry or world. When, instead of laughing at the strange and unusual, we embrace it and wonder how it could benefit all of us.

Steve is every man and every woman today—the loyal part, the part that still wants to do what he or she is told, that wants to please parents and bosses, and that wants things to stay the same. But they won't. And we must change with them or be left behind. To not move ahead now is to move behind. And be left there. The familiar and habitual are all enticing, and their attraction is so great that unless we have a dream—not just a sketchy one but one fully developed in Technicolor, filled with the sound and fury of emotion and desire—it is not likely that we will escape their gravitational force.

Steve may have had to disappoint his dad and withstand the stares and whispers of everyone who thought he had it made. But Steve was fortunate in a usually unnoticed and unappreciated way... his second divorce fractured his life and laid it open to look at and feel newly.

He was fortunate he didn't rely on drugs and alcohol to numb his job-claustrophobia and deaden his passionate desires. Fortunate he had enough money to have the freedom to make changes. Fortunate he had the self-confidence to not just preview his dream that day at Wendy's, but to follow it and stand up for it even when it seemed to be failing. And fortunate that strep throat and his loyalty to his son kept him home for a week... those precious few days that allowed Steve to think and wonder and plan and change.

When such an opportunity presents itself, will you have the wisdom to seize it?

"Creativity rarely happens in the workplace: Only one in three (34 percent) rate the workplace as one of their top three locations for creativity. During the commute (34 percent), in the shower or bath (25 percent) or during exercise (22 percent) are other favored places and times for inspiration."

Creativity Under Threat: No Time to Talk About It
September 25, 2013 PRNewswire New York

Baby Boomers...Retired and Bored to Tears

I knew I'd be one of the first Baby Boomers to retire, but receiving my first social security check is a real shocker! Dave thought as he tore open the U.S. Government envelope his mailman just handed him.

Heaven knows Dave had paid his "societal dues." He served his tour of duty in Vietnam, lost two fingers to friendly fire, and received an honorable discharge. After the war, Dave returned home to Columbus and had married his college sweetheart who had written every day and eagerly awaited his return. Dave and Lillian started Starlight Cleaners and worked it together as they raised their girls. When Starlight Cleaners sold two years ago, Dave and Lillian imagined how shocked they would have been back then to receive this three million dollar check. They gave each daughter a half million and invested the rest so they would be able to enjoy the future they had worked so long and hard to fund. Dave and Lillian had only one concern.

Their daughters Pat and Dolly were divorced and raising kids. Lillian always had Dave there to parent with her, and she was worried about her daughters' ability to parent alone. Dave consoled Lillian saying, "Well, my dear, our girls worked in the business with us so we've been able to pass on some business skills and give them a financial leg up as well. After completing the sale of their family home, they headed for Tampa and bought a three bedroom condo there so their daughters and grandkids would be able to come and stay with them in Florida.

Then they moved to the next item on their Retirement Dream List. They rented a travel van and headed west to San Francisco, down U.S. 1 to Los Angeles and San Diego. For the next five months they enjoyed every Indian Reservation, museum, and state capital along the way. Returning to Florida, they settled into retirement the way they had imagined it. Dave took his small boat out and fished every morning. Lillian spent those hours plowing through the pile of romance novels she had been looking forward to reading for years. They went shopping or to a movie in the afternoon, enjoyed dinner around 6:00, watched TV till 10:00 and headed to bed. No demands. No pressures. Whew, what a life!

The first year Pat, Dolly and the kids came for Thanksgiving and Christmas. But then soccer games and school events made scheduling difficult and their visits became less frequent. Three years into retirement, Dave and Lillian were drinking more than their usual occasional cocktail, sleeping later and longer, doing less and getting on each others' nerves. "What's happened to us?" Lillian asked one morning at breakfast. And Dave quickly responded, "We're obsessed with early-bird specials and grocery coupons we don't need."

Looking over his reading glasses and newspaper, Dave stated flatly, "The problem is we're bored... bored to tears. For 40 years our lives were demanding and full. We had kids to look after, employees to coach, clients to satisfy, our business and community to improve. Now nobody needs us. It had seemed like Nirvana at first but Dave and Lillian had come to the same conclusion, "If this is retirement, we don't want any more of it!"

The following Sunday Dave saw an article in the paper. It said that a large number of divorced and unmarried mothers in the area desperately needed help — legal help to protect their kids, job help to pay their bills, and emotional help to handle their day to day pressures and responsibilities. Mature volunteers were needed. A phone number was provided.

Ten days later, Lillian and Dave were seated on the hard wooden chairs at the Department of Welfare listening to case worker Judy Brookes. "You will need to visit your family twice a week. Elsie is a single mom with a four-year old named John. Elsie's husband left for work one day and never returned. She is overwhelmed, unhappy and alone, and she needs you to help her set goals and teach her the skills she will need to pursue them and raise a successful son at the same time. Gee, thought Lillian, this sounds familiar! Dave's mind raced back to raising his daughters and making Starlight Cleaners successful. His energy surged. Lillian's heart raced.

A month later, Dave and Lillian returned to the Welfare Office to meet Elsie and John. Lillian immediately wanted to take them home and mother them, but they both knew that wasn't what was needed. Instead Dave helped Elsie start a budget so she could do a better job of making the minimum-wage salary she was earning as a janitor at the local high school last through the month. Lillian took Elsie to a thrift store and showed her how to buy high-quality used clothes. Dave brought over a fish he caught one morning and Lillian showed Elsie how to make a nourishing stew. They brainstormed how Elsie could cut down fast foods and eat a healthy diet inexpensively. They helped her create a resume and taught her how to make calls to obtain reference letters. Together they searched for a job with greater benefits and higher pay.

Their twice weekly visits with Elsie and John became a vital part of their lives. Dave and Lillian looked forward to each opportunity to teach them the skills they would need. They loved hearing each detail of how John's grades were climbing and each comment by Elsie that proved she was more in charge of her life. The resume writing paid off. Elsie landed a grounds management job at the local university with a much higher salary, health benefits, and the opportunity to take free classes toward her degree. Elsie and John were healthier and far more self-confident. They were using the skills they would need to lead successful lives, and Dave and Lillian knew they had made a difference, not just in Elsie's life but in John's... and the family he would one day father and lead.

At dinner a year later, Dave observed, "Unlike the first three years of retirement, this year has been wonderful. And Lillian chimed in, "You should write an article for AARP magazine. Other retirees need to know what's ahead that's fulfilling... and what will bore them to tears. "Good idea, I'll do just that. Let's see what our generation still has in it to give!" he said with a chuckle.

It's time to update your dream for the future

Unlike many Baby Boomers, Lillian and Dave had arrived at retirement with more than enough money. They were able to do whatever they wanted, but their "old thinking about retirement" had them trapped. For years they had looked forward to finally being able to "do little or nothing" — no getting up early, no driving to work in traffic, no phone calls, and no one else's needs to be responsible for. But what they didn't realize was how important these typically annoying aspects of life really are. They had arrived at their dream but, once there, they didn't want it.

Many Baby Boomers update their ideas about retirement out of necessity, but it's important to keep your dreams up to date... no matter what. In fact it may be a matter of life and death! Years ago Susan worked with a group of surgeons who told her they had noticed that patients with attractive dreams — the birth of a child or moving into a new home — seemed to come through surgeries with flying colors. But their patients who dreaded the future didn't fare as well. The will to live, they concluded, is rooted in people's dreams. Dreams are what keep us alive and moving ahead. Were Dave and Lillian simply bored to tears... or might they have become bored to death?

Lillian and Dave had spent their lives succeeding and leading in all three gears. Day after day they had been teaching these skills to their daughters, friends and coworkers. They had built their confidence and given them the independence and the 2nd Gear leadership they needed to become productive and efficient, to assume more responsibility and earn additional money. And Lillian and Dave had geared up into 3rd Gear whenever their daughters or team members had an idea that needed to be nurtured into implementation. They had not realized how fulfilling shifting gears... theirs' and others'... had been. Once people learn something new, it is natural to pass it on. Shifting up and down again with Elsie and John was giving Lillian and Dave a new lease on life.

The future of our society depends on our ability and willingness to model and teach what we've learned: Our challenges have brought solutions; our failures have brought improved methods; the problems we've helped people through have made us wiser coaches and counselors. This accumulation of life-experience has a life of its own—a life we must nurture by using and sharing it.

Unlike Lillian and Dave, instead of selling their businesses and stepping out altogether, many owners are moving into a consulting role and staying involved part-time. Today's technology allows them to be reached by email or phone—unless they're scaling mountains or surveying the ruins of Machu Picchu. The fulfillment derived from continuing to Co-dream and contribute is not only enlivening to the company but also to its owner.

Whether consulting will work for you or not will depend on how effectively you have prepared your team in all three gears. Receiving an excessive number of frantic calls is a signal they are still dependent on you (stuck in 1st and 2nd Gears) and unprepared to take over. "Be sure your training programs go beyond job-related skills. Provide training in leadership, management and other career-building areas. All this training creates worker loyalty, something you will need if other companies try to snatch your employees away," writes Suzanne Martin in *Self-Employed America*.

"In one of the broadest efforts so far to link the nation's aging work force with available jobs, **AARP and Home Depot** Inc. are forming a national hiring partnership."

Dow Jones Newswires February 6, 2004

Dreaming Beyond AIDS

One would imagine that being a professional fundraiser was a glamorous job... wining and dining major donors, organizing functions and outings, one round of fun events after another. But it was far more than that. Brenda Samson knew the perils of fickle benevolent donors who loved you one minute and dropped you the next. Last year, she and her hardworking staff of three had raised over $6,000,000 for a prestigious Manhattan hospital, but according to the Board of Directors, it wasn't enough. The $45,000 salary barely covered Brenda's necessities. However she had a rent-controlled apartment and a kind-hearted boyfriend who had exited the corporate sector to create his walk-your-dog business which netted $150,000 a year. Despite the perils and low salary, the work was exciting for Brenda. There was the constant challenge of who to approach and which hallway or doorway would be named for a donor. Unlike Jobs and Benefits, there were no rules to follow. You created your own way or you failed. Every minute, every phone call, every contact brought the unexpected.

One day, a call came in that would transform Brenda's life. A charity with a $15 million budget, Fight World Aids, was looking for a new director. Brenda was being considered for the position. She would have a staff of thirty-five, Business Class world travel, and a $200,000 a year salary, and when her feet touched the ground, she realized she'd been in training for this job her entire life.

During the final interview, a panel of twelve decision-makers grilled Brenda for two hours. They fired question after question and Brenda impressed them. She had the right background and academically she had the right stuff. She had graduated from Harvard, was a member of the Harvard Club, and could give the Harvard handshake, an attribute the committee considered important to opening doors and finding key people. The fact that she was a Rhodes Scholar and had a degree from Oxford clinched the deal.

With 50 million HIV positive individuals worldwide, Brenda would have to think at a whole new level. This wasn't asking a donor to place their name on a hospital wing for $20,000; it was asking The Gates Foundation for $50 million. Her first month on the job was a powerful learning experience. Brenda spent two days in every department studying each aspect of the work they did. She listened; she asked; she moved ahead step by step until she fully understood how the organization worked. Fight World Aids had three objectives: create global awareness of the plight of HIV positive people, generate publicity, and bring in donations.

Brenda put together a panel of fifteen who were outstanding in the world community and began Co-dreaming with them. During a weekend retreat in the Hamptons, they created a shared vision of the world beyond aids, a world where, like polio, AIDS rarely occurs and is readily treated. They developed a detailed strategy for getting from here to there. The approach they agreed upon was a competition called Our Story. In line with their mission, first, they would invite HIV-positive people worldwide to send in essays, photos and poems telling their stories in detail: who they are; what they were doing before they contracted AIDS; and what they are doing now to cope with the disease.

The panel realized that to make the changes in funding and treatment that would be needed, they would have to bring AIDS out of the unconscious hidden compartment in which most people have it stored... it's over there, in them but it has no effect on me, my family or friends. The strategy entailed educating people that AIDS is a disease that impacts all of us and that all of us must solve. From the entries, the judges would select 50 essays, 50 photos and 50 poems and the winners' submissions would become part of an exhibition they would present around the world. Initially the exhibition would be in English and then it would be translated into other languages. Winning entries would be published in a book called Our Story. Proceeds from the exhibition and the sale of the book would go to Fight World AIDS. A presentation would be available free of charge on their website.

The scope of the Our Story project tested every inch of Brenda and her team's skills, abilities and creativity. Once the board approved it, they immediately went to work. It was a massive undertaking which required detailed planning, broad-outreach marketing, and the creation of a network of volunteers in 40 countries. The vision would need to be shared in detail; rules would have to be established and constantly updated; judges would have to be appointed and over 80,000 entries evaluated before the final 150 winners would be chosen.

The project quickly took on a life of its own. Its website began communicating Our Story's progress in over 40 languages. The media became powerful champions. Over 150 magazines and 6,000 newspapers followed its progress and broadcast its message worldwide. The Our Story campaign won awards before it was completed. It was a cause whose time had come.

Eight months later, the winning works were reaching the world. Five exhibits were traveling simultaneously. The website was getting 200,000 hits a day. Three books about the project had been published. And, most important of all, over $300 million in revenue had been generated from books sales, exhibition fees, and donations. The plight of AIDS sufferers — their stories, photos and poems — were touching the hearts of millions and making us all aware that together we can move beyond AIDS.

Three-Gear Leaders will change the world

Yes, Brenda could have ignored that phone call and missed this opportunity, telling herself the job was too big or she didn't have enough experience. But instead she greased her gears and took it on masterfully. This is what we will all need to do in the years ahead.

The workplace has changed and we must change with it. The pace of life and work is continuing to accelerate and, fortunately, the opportunities to be creative and innovative are accelerating as well. Brenda's boyfriend was able to support her when she was working for the hospital because of his dog-walking business designed to meet the needs of people who treasure their dogs but don't have time to walk them. No, that wasn't what Eric had expected to be doing when he was the vice-president of a Silicon Valley startup several years ago, but that's what works for him now.

What opportunities do you see around you... like the one Marge discovered in her class and brought to fruition with her husband Harry? Or the one Charles and his Indian counterpart Dalal discovered when their jobs were threatened and they formed their own firm? What passions do you have that might translate into a job the way Phil's love of cars had with his wife Audrey's support? What is pressuring you to change the way Pete did when he purchased a Cruise Away franchise? What is holding your business back that you need to change, the way Max Kim did when he brought us in to train his managers? Or, like the Barron family, what issues are confronting you at home that you need to shift gears to lead more skillfully? Or are you, like the Red Firecracker, someone who can go in and transform a hotel or a business? Or like Christine Martindale who can come up with an idea like "designer flowers" that will take your business beyond the stresses of competition?

What impact are leaders around you having in your life? Which ones are working to keep you in 1st Gear—stuck in outdated rules and regulations—like those who stayed for their paychecks in Marvin's Jobs and Benefits organization? Who is constantly pushing you to produce more even though the methods and systems aren't capable of eking out any more-better-faster-cheaper no matter how long or hard you push? What signals are you getting that you and your organization are overusing 2nd Gear? What integrity issues are you noticing? What new skills and technologies are failing to be learned? What creative ideas are being ignored? And who is giving you feedback that you're going too long and hard? Is it your spouse or your kids? Or is your body signaling that it can't take it anymore. That, do or die, you must make changes NOW?

"Some men see things as they are and say, 'Why?'
I dream of things that never were and say, 'Why not?'"

Robert F. Kennedy

Max Kim of Ace Computers

The setting was luxurious—the conference room at the Mandarin Hotel in Hong Kong. Waiters in white gloves were delivering impeccable service. The room had been immaculately set up. No detail had been overlooked or considered too small. Even the china coffee cups with their tiny silver spoons had been placed in neat rows on white, stiffly-starched, linen table clothes. Fresh flowers adorned the room.

Max Kim wanted to drive home a point to his 20 Southeast Asia sales executives: "Take every detail of this two-day training seriously! This is the sales strategy we will need to increase our market share."

Max, VP of Sales for the USA, Southeast Asia and South Africa, was 37 but he still looked 18. Short with a boyish grin he was a powerhouse at this global computer giant. He was responsible for 55 sales directors around the world and spent 90% of his time traveling.

When Max stood up to introduce us, he began, "It is essential that you understand why I have gathered you all here today. Several months ago on a plane, I read Susan Ford Collins's book *The Joy of Success* and I had one of those moments we rarely experience in a lifetime, when the power of an 'Aha!' leaves us electrified and changed. When I read Chapter Two, *Using All 3 Success Gears, Not Just 1 or 2*, I understood why our approach to selling major accounts simply wasn't working. I immediately emailed Susan and registered for a two-day workshop she and Richard were conducting in Miami, *Three Gears of Successful Leadership: What's Gone Wrong in the Workplace and What You Can Do About It*. At their suggestion, I arrived a day early so they could learn about our business needs in more detail," Max added.

When Max arrived, we quickly discovered what a skillful leader he was. The first thing he did was show us the mission statement he'd written for his sales executives: Through Exceptional Leadership We Create the World's Best Computer Sales Team. "Leadership is vital," Max told us."We can't grow our business without leaders and, Susan, I've never seen leadership explained as simply and completely as you did in your book. When these two days are over, I want you to also teach your skills to my sales executives in Johannesburg and Chicago. You will be my team's mentors from now on."

"Sales people frequently get stuck in 2nd Gear, "Max continued. "They do anything to make the sale but then are unable to gear down to meet the 1st Gear needs of their customers. 2nd Gear responses to 1st Gear needs are a mismatch. This is the biggest problem I see in selling today, in all industries and with our own vendors. We lose business because we can't handle the basics. Our sales teams on three continents are stuck in 2nd Gear and we can't get them out of it. Our managers pressure salespeople to close instead of taking time up front to discover the details of our clients' needs and requirements, the details of their information manuals, the specifics of their systems and the solutions they seek. So, not only do they fail to gear up into the vision but, because they're racing and revving, they fail to gear down into 1st Gear as well."

"For example, Max added, "South African Airways (SAA) asks us to bid on a contract for 300 computer terminals. And what happens? First, our Johannesburg sales team writes and presents the proposal. Meanwhile, SAA asks our two main competitors to bid on these terminals as well so then we are all bidding for the same business. Here's where we come up short. Once our initial proposal has been delivered, SAA begins asking for changes. SAA wants a sample of what our long-term working relationship will be like. They're in 1st Gear, and they want to know whether we can shift into 1st with them. Do we listen to their needs in detail and meet them precisely? Do we take time to explain how our product and system work so they can integrate them with other systems they have in place? Do we get back to them on time with information they request? Are we skillful and effective in our follow through and delivery? Can we work as an integrated team? And what they find out is… we can't.

Instead our sales managers rush in and pressure their teams to start selling. They think they can win business by lowering prices and promising terms we can't deliver. Of course, in the end we don't get the deal. Or we do, and it turns out to be a nightmare. It's a typical 2nd Gear strategy. What is the outcome? Our salespeople become frustrated and leave or our managers fire them. They don't realize how much time, money and, most of all, good will that strategy costs us. I need you to teach them that a good leader is in 1st Gear with his team first. Once they have gained the necessary product knowledge and confidence, they can move ahead into 2nd Gear… but not before. Some of these contracts are worth hundreds of millions of dollars and we're working on ten to twenty contracts a day. This is big business," Max emphasized, "and we've got to get this right… fast. With your three gears in mind, we can more clearly see the vital leadership role our sales director plays. He or she must, as you say, be able to operate in all three gears and shift up and down as needed. When we get this right, we can seize the business opportunities that come our way."

You can't grow your business without leaders

We were immediately struck by how smart, in all three gears, Max Kim really was. It was obvious why he was being groomed to be president.

What the Ace Computers story tells us is that no matter how good your product is, without the right sales force, you don't stand a chance. And, if you don't have the right managers, your sales force doesn't have a chance either. We have worked with sales teams for the last 30 years so we know firsthand how crucial effective leadership is. We have watched businesses come and go simply because the leaders lacked vision and an understanding of how and when to use the gears. Whether it's an international computer business or a local car dealer, the success and leadership principles apply.

As Max said, you can't grow your business without leaders. Many people think leaders are born and not made. But nothing could be further from the truth. Leadership is something you can learn and master. Some of the best schools in the country, such as the University of Chicago's Graduate School of Business, are already teaching these gear-shifting skills to the next generation of business leaders.

As the global competition heats up, leadership skills, in all three gears, play a more crucial role in our lives. Those who succeed and thrive will be able to see when their jobs are going away and observe current needs and create new products, services and businesses to meet them. Erica L. Groshen, a labor economist at the Federal Reserve Bank of New York said, "As we trade, we release more labor from the service sector because our highly skilled and highly paid workers lose their competitive advantage. So we go on to the next big thing. We specialize in innovation. We start new products and industries."

No matter how well educated and experienced you are, outside forces can compel you to start over at any moment. But will you have the courage and skills to do that... successfully?

"In 2004, "we reshaped GE values around four core actions: Imagine, Solve, Build and Lead. Imagine at GE is the freedom to dream and the power to make it real. Solve reflects GE's unique ability to tackle the world's toughest problems. Build requires a performance culture that creates customer and shareholder value. Lead reflects our spirit of optimism that embraces change, and our values of openness and energy; it's what it will take to win."

Jeffrey R. Immelt
Chairman of the Board and CEO
General Electric

Afterword: With the Outcome Clearly in Mind

Question: In these times that are filled with changes and challenges, who will have what it takes to seize the opportunities that abound?
Answer: The individuals and organizations that can use All Three Success and Leadership Gears… at the right time… will be ready and able. Those who cannot will become more and more frustrated and out of sync.

Most people don't realize that success and leadership have three gear-like phases. Like gears in a car, you must know how and when to shift them. If you use the wrong gear at the wrong time, then no matter how hard you work or how many hours you put in, you will be unable to make headway in today's world. Unfortunately most people, like most drivers, rely on automatic transmissions to shift their gears for them. But our "societal transmissions" were designed for a very different time so they are failing to shift us up and down as needed, and we are feeling the consequences in our health, careers and families. When individuals and organizations *unconsciously* rely on others to shift their gears for them — parents, teachers, bosses and other authority figures — they are unable to understand why some people get "all the breaks" and they don't; why their long hours and hard work fail to produce the outcomes they desire; why some individuals, organizations and countries blossom and thrive while others stall and fail.

Highly successful people have learned to sense precisely when each gear is needed, and they can quickly and flexibly shift up and down to reach the destinations they choose. In *Success Has Gears*, we have shared the cues, signals and timings they use… so you can use them too.

As we pursue our careers and dreams, we can no longer afford to use the wrong gear at the wrong time. Nor can we afford to have leaders who are stuck in the wrong gear, squeezing the life out of their organizations and employees. We are rapidly moving into a society in which we, as individuals, will need to make more decisions than ever before, about health, education and finances, which career to pursue, what new skills and retraining we will need. A society in which we must shift gears more and more frequently and effectively.

What is success? This is a vital question. To be fulfilling, our definition of success must be updated to include all three gears. First, it must encompass health, security, values, self-confidence, education and skills.. Second, it must include productivity and satisfying, rewarding work. And, third, success must include time for creativity and dreams, for invention and discovery; it must incorporate rest, recreation, and quality time with family and friends.

When Susan spent time with renowned world-futurist Buckminster Fuller years ago, he saw the world quite differently than other people do. He saw us living on Spaceship Earth, journeying through the universe cycle by cycle. We are Earth's crew, he said, responsible for tending our planet and one another, for managing its resources and environment.

"Think of it. We are blessed with technology that would be indescribable to our forefathers. We have the wherewithal, the know-it-all to feed everybody, clothe everybody, and give every human on Earth a chance. We know now what we could never have known before—that we now have the option for all humanity to "make it" successfully on this planet in this lifetime."

Buckminster Fuller 1980

What are the problems we face today as individuals and as a society? In good times and in bad times, in sickness and in health, we are now "married" to our global neighbors. If we teamed up and worked together in all three gears, what global solutions could we then generate?

Could we deliver a healthcare system that meets not only the needs of our country but the needs of our global population—a population that is constantly flying in and out of America; that is growing our food, manufacturing the products we use, and becoming an integral part of our businesses and lives?

Could we give the next generation an educational system that will prepare them to succeed in their world, a world that may be quite different from the one we know today? Can we prepare the existing workforce to thrive in this rapidly changing environment and can we develop leaders who nurture productivity and innovation within their companies, industries and communities?

Can we pass on an up-to-date infrastructure: roads, airports, tunnels and bridges? Can we become more conscious of our need to assure the health and wellbeing of our planet's environment? Can we learn how to communicate and cooperate with people and countries to create balanced and peaceful lives?

These are our challenges. And—with All Three Gears of Success and Leadership in place, and our outcome clearly in mind—these are our opportunities day by day, at work and at home.

Susan Ford Collins and Richard Israel
www.technologyofsuccess.com

Acknowledgments

As we chatted after speaking at the MegaSuccess Conference, we suddenly realized, "These stories are a book!" In the months that followed, we spent hours in daily meetings punctuated by walks around Susan's koi pond and lunches at Maleewan and nights overflowing with ideas and emails back and forth. But completing *Success Has Gears* wasn't something we could do all by ourselves. Many people dreamed this dream with us and lent us their support and expertise.

Sarah Caldicott, co-author of *Innovate Like Edison*, played a major leadership role. She introduced us to the *Spherion Emerging Workforce Study* and arranged for us to meet Robert Morgan and his staff.

Many people in many locations have read the manuscript and given us vital input via phone and internet: Dilip Mukerjea in Singapore, Cliff Shaffron in Hong Kong, Stuart Elliott in London, Al Homyk, Gwen Carden, Max Kamine, Dr. Bernie Cleveland and Kathy Shurte across the U.S.

Besides those who reviewed *Success Has Gears* online, a large group of individuals came to Susan's home and read to us... out loud... as long as they could. (If you've ever read to your kids, you know how exhausting that is.) We watched and listened for the places in the text where they hesitated or asked questions and we made corrections. Thanks to Penny Steele, John Ventiera, Sheila Clarke, Leslie Loewenthal and Linda Fine. Sharon Huff contributed not only her design savvy but her love and enthusiasm to birthing the book. Our appreciation to Dennis Collins who read to us from the head of the boardroom table at Jefferson Pilot Communications. And a bouquet of red roses to Mara Reuben who spent an entire weekend reading out loud and giving valuable input. Whew, what commitment!

The stories in this book are contagious. People kept saying "this reminds me of ..." They asked us to email this story or that to a friend "who is in the same situation and needs to read it and the solutions you've provided immediately!"

Special thanks to Robert Morgan, Jim Coker, Elizabeth Smith, Kip Havel and Marcy Potts at Spherion for their work on the Foreword. To Jack Scarborough, Dean of the Business School at Barry University, for his keen observations and insights. To Janet Carabelli for holding the vision of transforming the workplace with these understandings. And to Penny Steele for her energy and support.

We are grateful to The Strategic Forum in Miami and New York for the people we met as the result of our participation in this powerful business networking organization.

As we neared completion, Richard's daughter Lana combed the manuscript for details we had long since become too big-picture oriented to notice. Thanks to Lois, Richard's partner, for her love, patience and support over the years.

Susan's beloved partner, Albert, was our tech guru, there to answer questions and find solutions till late in the night, creating styles and unraveling the mysteries of tables. *The Technology of Success Book Series* became our shared labor of love.

A very special thank you to Kristen McLean for sourcing and inspiring the 2014 Technology of Success Book Series and to Tim Kordik for designing the covers.

About the Authors: Susan Ford Collins

S usan Ford Collins is the creator of *The Technology of Success*. She has facilitated over 3,000 training programs for executive, management, human resources, sales and customer service teams in prestigious business institutions such as American Express, IBM, Florida Power & Light, Kimberly-Clark, Digital, Ryder System, Merrill Lynch, CondeNast, and Coopers and Lybrand. She has spoken in educational organizations across the country. After two appearances on CNN, Lou Dobbs invited her to teach *The Technology of Success* to his entire Financial News Team.

"Susan was the keynote speaker at our *Profiles of Excellence* awards banquet honoring Wendy's founder Dave Thomas's wife Lorraine. Dave was sitting next to Susan at the head table. He'd had heart surgery weeks before and all through the evening, Lorraine fed him slowly like a child—he didn't greet anyone in anything but a flat murmur. He was obviously still in great pain. But when Susan finished speaking, Dave rose to his feet and threw his arms around her with tears in his eyes. This is the power Susan has as a speaker."
Yvette Diana, Chairperson, *Profiles of Excellence*

Over the years Susan's audiences begged her to write so they could share what they learned with families and co-workers, and learn more themselves. Their pleas led Susan to write *The Technology of Success Book Series*.

The Technology of Success Book Series...
Book One... *The Joy of Success: 10 Essential Skills for Getting the Success You Want*, Susan Ford Collins

"I have been reading books on success for over 30 years. This is one of the most sophisticated and useful ones I have ever read. I highly recommend it."
Jack Canfield, coauthor *Chicken Soup for the Soul*

Book Two... *Success Has Gears: Using the Right Gear at the Right Time in Business and Life*, Susan Ford Collins and Richard Israel

"A thought-provoking guide to the dynamic process of leading in the modern workplace—even when you are simply leading yourself to higher levels of performance."
Greg Horn, CEO, General Nutrition Centers

Book Three...*Our Children Are Watching: 10 Skills for Leading the Next Generation to Success*, Susan Ford Collins

"I read hundreds of books every year and I can count on one hand how many books I have ever read that hold the potential to transform lives as deeply as this book does. Without any hesitation, I give *Our Children Are Watching* my absolute HIGHEST recommendation. Whether you read it for yourself or for your children, it has the power to change your life forever, if you are willing."

Review, Chinaberry Book Service

"A book full of hope—a very valuable item."
Michael Fitzsimmons, Producer *The Weekend Today Show*

Book Four... *The Miracle Diet: Lose Weight, Gain Health: 10 Diet Skills, ,* Susan Ford Collins and Celso Cukierkorn

Why is this diet book different? Diets fail not because you don't know what or how much to eat. Diets fail because it takes 10 Success Skills to overcome the challenges of changing habits.

Like it or not, we're all on a diet, whether it includes eating a bag of chips or an apple! The question is... are you on a diet that will make you and your family sick, or make you all well?

susanfordcollins@msn.com or www.technologyofsuccess.com

About the Authors: Richard Israel

Richard Israel is the author and co-author of numerous other books including *Your Mind At Work, How to THINK Creatively, Sales Genius, The Brainsmart Leader, Supersellf, The Vision,* and *Brain $ell.* His work has been translated into over 25 languages and acclaimed by international media, including *Business Week, Success Magazine, The New York Sunday Times* and *The South China Morning Post.*

Richard is a consultant, speaker and trainer with over 40 years of international expertise in sales training, leadership, and strategies for coping with information overload. His clients include GlaxoSmithKline, British Airways USA, International Distillers & Vinters United Kingdom, Royal & Sunalliance Hong Kong, Turner Broadcasting Southeast Asia, Nassau Marriott Resort–Bahamas, Zurich, Argentina, Plate Glass Republic of South Africa, Guangxi Yuchai Machinery China, and Rouse USA.

More than one and a half million people across four continents have participated in his programs. He has coached companies in retail, hospitality, airline, automobile, manufacturing, government and the service sector to achieve increased sales and productivity. Richard resides in Miami, Florida.

Other books by Richard Israel

Brainsell, Tony Buzan and Richard Israel, McGraw Hill

An international bestseller.
The first whole creative brain sales training book. Now in 25 languages.

The BrainSmart Leader, Tony Buzan, Richard Israel and Tony Dottino, Gower Publishing
"The tools in this book give leaders everything they need to tackle today's complex business problems."
Rich Bannon, Senior VP and Corporate Controller
Entex Information Services

Grass Roots Leaders, Tony Buzan, Richard Israel and Tony Dottino, Gower Publishing
"I have been waiting 30 years for this book and it arrived at the very time I was designing an Executive MBA Course in Leadership. This book will become foundation reading."

Stephen C. Lundin, PhD, author of *FISH!* **books and** *Top Performer*

How to THINK Creatively Using the "TILS" 4 Step Technique, Richard Israel and Conni Gordon, Winterstreet

"A most helpful guide for parents, as well as busy business executives."
Dr. Abby Ross, Psychologist

Your Mind at Work, Richard Israel, Helen Whitten and Cliff Shaffran, Kogan Page Publishers

"A wealth of creative ideas and strategies to develop self-knowledge in the business arena."
Professor Bill Ford, Southern Cross University
New South Wales, Australia

Mind Chi: Re-wire Your Brain in 8 Minutes a Day, Richard Israel and Vanda North. Capstone/Wiley

"8 minute daily dose of Mind Chi will improve vitality and reduce stress."
Stephen C. Lundin, PhD, author *FISH* **books and** *Top Performer*

Sales Genius, Tony Buzan and Richard Israel. Gower Publishing

"A Master Class in selling"
Jonathan Norman, Publisher

MetaMind Yoga, Richard Israel with Margo Berman, Kindle

"Every chapter fills you with good vibes and positive energy."
Natalie Sultan, amazon reader

brainsell@aol.com or www.technologyofsuccess.com

Made in the USA
Middletown, DE
21 August 2023

36767275R00087